GOLDSMITH
and
SENTIMENTAL COMEDY

B.S. PATHANIA
Chairman, Dept. of English
H.P. University
SHIMLA

PRESTIGE
PRESTIGE BOOKS
NEW DELHI

GOLDSMITH AND SENTIMENTAL COMEDY

Price: Rs. 120

First Published: 1988

Published by:
Prestige Books
3/28, East Patel Nagar
New Delhi 110 008
Phone: 5710787

Printed by:
Creative Printers
W.Z. 130-A, Naraina
New Delhi 110 028

For my wife

Contents

Preface

Though much has been written about Oliver Goldsmith as a comic dramatist, there has been surprisingly little in the way of really close and systematic examination of his comedies in the context of sentimental comedy which was a popular, if not the dominant, form of drama in the eighteenth century. Several critics have put Goldsmith on the sentimental bench by greatly exaggerating the resemblances and ignoring the differences between his comedies and those of the sentimental school. In their anxiety to prove the dominance of sentimental comedy they have greatly underrated the unsentimentalism of Goldsmith as a playwright. In order to restore a correct perspective, I have tried to lay special emphasis on the gay and anti-sentimental nature of his comedies, *The Good-Natur'd Man* and *She Stoops to Conquer*.

The first three chapters of this study attempt to show not only the rise of sentimental comedy in reaction to the Restoration comedy of manners but also the real nature of sentimental comedy which harmonized with the contemporary ethos. Chapter 4 reveals the theoretical opposition of Goldsmith to sentimental comedy, as shown by his critical remarks scattered in his major works. Chapters 5 and 6 attempt an almost scene-wise analysis of his comedies to show that their spirit is antithetical to that of sentimental comedy. An attempt has also been made in these two chapters to defend Goldsmith's comedies against some specific, though misguided, charges of sentimentality by questioning some judgements and confirming others.

The scholarly work of Nettleton, Bernbaum, Nicoll, Sherbo and Quintana lays a heavy debt on all students of eighteenth-century drama. I have acknowledged this debt at several points in the body of the text. I wish to record my special indebtedness to Professor Ferguson of Duke University, Durham, North Carolina, for his useful help and guidance in the preparation of my chapters on Goldsmith. And, finally, I am grateful to my wife Sarla for her constant encouragement throughout the course of this study.

B.S. Pathania

1

Introduction

Some critics have claimed that the Restoration comedy of manners is marked by profundity and high seriousness. For example, Dale Underwood observes that it deals with "problems fundamental not only to the seventeenth century but to the nature of man."[1] The detractors of this comedy, on the other hand, have tried to show that its concerns are "trivial, gross and dull."[2] Such conflicting views depend upon generalizations that do not hold good for the output of the entire Restoration period.

It is not correct to say that the Restoration comedy of manners is concerned with the quest for reality or presenting any profound ideas, or probing character deeply. While it does reflect social and intellectual issues of the time, it primarily aims at entertainment. Congreve's Belmour in *The Old Bachelor* (1693) aptly voices its spirit: "Come, come, leave Business to Idlers, and Wisdom to Fools. . . . Wit, be my Faculty, and Pleasure, my Occupation: and let Father Time shake his Glass." Such comedy owes its nature to the actual life of the upper class that it depicts. The code of behaviour expressed in this witty, gay, cynical and "immoral" comedy was the code actually operative in the court of Charles II. As "the drama's laws the drama's patrons give," this comedy could hardly have been anything but what it is. Macaulay seems to ignore this fact in his well-known essay which severely censures the comic dramatists of the Restoration period.

The Restoration comedy does not, however, depict the society as a whole in the modern sense. It is now generally recognized that not the whole nation was impregnated with the spirit of the dissolute court of Charles II. Even in his day people flocked in their thousands to the churches to hear the sermons of men like South, Barrow and Stillingfleet. Also, it was in this age that Bunyan's *Pilgrim's Progress* was so popular that by 1688 its ten editions had been sold. The middle classes still lived as decent lives as they had done during the Commonwealth. But they were not yet in a position to determine the course of drama, as the Restoration had placed supreme power in the hands of the merry King, the chief patron of the early Restoration playwrights.

The life at the court was altogether different from life in the city as the latter was the stronghold of Puritanism. The Puritans had, of course, always regarded the drama and other forms of entertainment as the Devil's work. But in the Restoration period the powerful influence of the court made it impossible for the Puritans to protest effectively against the licentious comedy which received its nurture and inspiration from the court. That it was thus a class comedy accounts for its narrow interests and its partial vision of life. As the King and his courtiers were determined to enjoy to the full every available pleasure, they relished such plays as Wycherley's *The Country Wife* (1675) and Etherege's *The Man of Mode* (1676), containing scenes of lewd conversation, of husbands cuckolded, and of wives seduced.

Such a comedy flourished so long as its indecency could look for support and example at court. However, the Revolution of 1688 hastened the emergence of a new social and moral climate. It brought to an end the period in which monarchy had enjoyed the heyday of its glory. The power of the King was curtailed and he became the servant of the people.

Aristocracy in the old sense was almost dead. As Trevelyan observes, "The Whitehall of the Merry Monarch now lay in ruins, never to rise again."[3] The Revolution enabled the upper middle classes to rise into social prominence by exercising power and political influence. While their moral temperament remained subdued in the reign of Charles II, they had never really abjured their emotive powers, their deep-rooted needs and their instinctive respect for moral laws. They could not have possibly associated themselves with a stage that exhibited infidelity and profligacy. By giving them a new importance in government, the Revolution helped them to a voice in literary matters.

In his excellent study,[4] Professor Loftis has given a detailed account of the increasing importance of the bourgeois component in the audience after 1688. Books and theatre no longer remained an exclusive affair of the aristocracy. Soon it became possible for this great body of respectable Englishmen to assert its influence effectively against the corruption of the times as of the stage. It made a determined effort to reform the contemporary manners and morals and gave support to the reformers of the stage.

According to Burnet, even before the Revolution of 1688 there were certain Religious Societies which brought to the notice of magistrates the names of those who indulged in drunkenness, swearing and public indecency. A few years later on, they came to be called Societies for Reformation which worked for repressing verbal indecency or profaneness upon the stage. William and Queen Mary commanded all Justices and Sheriffs to execute the laws against lewdness, indecency and irreligion. Later Queen Anne issued a proclamation for the promotion of piety and morality.

In this general reform movement, opposition to the licentious stage was inevitable. But even before the Revolution of 1688, opposition was by no means entirely inactive. John Evelyn complained to Viscount Cornby in 1664: "You know, my Lord, that I . . . am far from Puritanism; but I would have no reproach left our adversaries in a thing which may so conveniently be reform'd. Plays are now with us become a licentious excess, and a vice, and need severe censors that should look as well to their morality, as to their lines and numbers."[5] Thomas Shadwell, in the preface to *The Sullen Lovers* (1668), wrote that "if there were nothing but the ill-manners of it, it should make poets avoid that indecent way of writing." In 1673 Richard Baxter, a presbyterian divine, complained that the plays of his age were "heinous aggravated sins."[6] Such sporadic attacks on the stage did not, however, count for much during the reign of Charles II when the influence of the court was strong.

After the Revolution, however, the climate of the age changed. A strong reaction against the indecency and immorality of the comedy of manners set in. Some even advocated a complete suppressing of the theatre. In the new climate the protests against the libertine ethic of the Restoration comedy gathered strength. But it was Jeremy Collier who encouraged the rallying of general opinion to the necessity of reform in comedy. In his *Short View of the Immorality and Profaneness of the English Stage* (1698) he denounced the comedy of manners for its immodesty, its profanity, its abuse of the clergy and its encouragement of immorality. He found in it "nothing but a little Whoring, Pimping, Gaming, Profaneness."[7]

The middle classes, known for their moral attitude to life and an instinctive preference for good sense over "small trifling forms," found at last their strident spokesman in Collier. His *Short View* condemned the Restoration playwrights for flouting all principles of conventional morality in their mode of expression. In his view, "goats and monkeys, if they could speak, would express their brutality in such language as this." An exponent of moral function of comedy, he remarked in the opening sentence of his *Short View* that the business of drama was to discourage vice and recommend virtue.

Collier achieved great success because his attack on the stage came at a time when a general movement for reformation of manners and morals, and for ethical attitude towards literature, had already started. Dr. Ward has shown how, after the *Short View*, the attitude of the law and government towards the stage showed a marked change:

> The censorship of the Master of the Revels began to be exercised more strictly; actors were prosecuted for the use of profane language, and the playhouses were once more presented as nuisances by the grand-jury; the admission of women wearing masks into any of the theatres was prohibited; and Convocation occupied itself with the condition of the stage as a matter of moment to be pressed upon the consideration of the Crown.[8]

As the Restoration comedy of manners was incapable of satisfying the moral and social needs of the age of William Anne, it provoked a reaction which gained in strength as the years went by. There was about the turn of the century a marked improvement in the tone of comedies. With the later Restoration playwrights the comedy of manners underwent a gradual transformation. The comedies of Southerne, Vanbrugh and Farquhar were remarkable for their freedom from coarseness and cynicism that marked the comedies of the early Restoration playwrights such as Dryden, Etherege and Wycherley. Even Congreve showed his awareness of the new demands of morality. His Mirabell in *The Way of the World* (1700) is different from the early Restoration heroes because of his relative sobriety and sententiousness. One has only to contrast him with Etherege's Dorimant in *The Man of Mode* or with Wycherley's Horner in *The Country Wife* to realize how different he is from the Restoration rake. He is, as Fujimura remarks, "the Restoration rake in the process of being transformed into a Wit of the age of sense and sensibility."[9] And another critic[10] even believes Mirabell to be an exemplary character.

Vanbrugh's gallants are much less wild and much more serious and sentimental than the earlier Restoration gallants. For example, his Heartfree in *The Provoked Wife* (1697) or Young Fashion in *The Relapse* (1696) is no match for Dorimant or Horner in rakishness. Heartfree thinks that "to be capable of loving one, doubtless is better than to possess a thousand." Surely this is an indictment of the licentious comedy of manners. Farquhar's characters, especially women, are as serious and moral as those of Vanbrugh. For example, his Angelica in *The Constant Couple* (1700) values real love, and not mere gallantry. Southerne's *The Wives' Excuse* (1691) adequately expresses the spirit of the closing years of the century. Its virtuous heroine, Mrs. Friendall, anticipates the heroines of the later sentimental comedy. Vanbrugh's Amanda in *The Relapse* is much different from gay heroines of the early Restoration comedy.

Anxious to meet the new demands of the middle-class public, Southerne, Vanbrugh and Farquhar endeavoured to achieve moral and sentimental effect. Their characters are much different from those of early Restoration playwrights whose heroes are notorious for their illicit amours, and the heroines for their coquetry. In the nineties there was a conscious attempt to moderate the tone of comedy by avoiding excessive indecency. The earlier intellectual, cynical and perverse comedy was gradually yielding place to a new kind of comedy that contained the elements of emotion, sentiment and moralizing. The new climate induced the playwrights to meet the demands of an increasingly bourgeois audience for such sentimental comedy.

Sentimental comedy came into being in reaction to the licentious comedy of manners and in response to the new ethos. It needs to be stressed that the sense in which "sentiment" was used in the eighteenth century was much different from our present habit of usage. In modern psychology, while "emotion" refers to feeling as it is actually experienced, "sentiment" denotes a disposition or tendency to feel emotions, but is not itself experienced. Leaving aside "sentiment" in this particular sense, it may be noted that in our own day the word and its derivatives are chiefly used in a derisive sense, implying insincerity, mawkishness and a shallow romantic, even unbalanced, emotional attitude. A sentimental person is supposed to express a greater degree of feeling than a specific situation warrants; he tends to lavish disproportionate emotion on trivial matters.

In the eighteenth century, however, "Sentiment"[11] was by no means a word of disparagement. Though it meant various things, it was mostly used in a favourable sense. For example, Dr. Johnson, in *Rambler* No. 37 (1750), used the term to denote an emotional thought: "Either the sentiments must sink to the level of speakers, or the speakers must be raised to the height of the sentiments." The *Oxford English Dictionary* quotes several other writers of the age to show that they used "sentiment" approvingly. Sterne, for example, is quoted as having written in 1768: " 'Tis the monarch of a people . . . so renown'd for sentiment and fine feelings, that I have to reason with." Sterne's contemporaries are shown as having used "sentiment" to mean "refined and tender emotion; exercise or manifestation of sensibility; emotional reflection or meditation."

In modern psychology "sentiment" is defined as an emotional disposition centring round the idea of an object, while "sensibility" denotes the capacity of being stimulated by sense stimuli The eighteenth century, however, was hardly conscious of any subtle distinction between the two terms. "Sensibility" then signified the power of feeling tender and refined emotions; of being moved by the pathetic in art and literature. This is best seen in the famous apostrophe to "Sensibility" in Sterne's *Sentimental Journey* (1768): "Dear Sensibility: source inexhausted of all that's precious in our joys, or costly in our sorrows !" Sheridan used this term to suggest refined taste and feeling. In the opening scene of *The School for Scandal*, Joseph says to Lady Sneerwell, "Madam, it is impossible for me to suspect a man of Mr. Snake's sensibility and discernment." The word was also used to convey acuteness of apprehension or feeling Addison, for example, wrote in *Spectator* No. 231: "Modesty . . . is a kind of quick and delicate Feeling in the Soul. . . .It is such an exquisite Sensibility, as warns a woman to shun the first Appearance of everything which is hurtful." Dr. Johnson's *Dictionary* (1755) gives "quickness of perception" among the meanings of the word.

Thus "sentiment" and "sensibility" meant almost one and the same thing in the eighteenth century. These terms were actually used by the writers of the period as interchangeable and synonymous. The sentimental comedy of the age, therefore, has sometimes been termed "comedy of sensibility."[12] Even in the history of the word "sensibility" is closely associated with that of "sentiment". Both came from France where sensibility was cultivated as a fine art before it became fashionable in England. Security of life, more leisure, and relatively stable culture in the eighteenth century proved conducive to the birth of a delicacy of sensation and a sensitiveness to the claims of others. Consequently, human sympathies had a remarkably wide expansion. A man of sentiment or sensibility was supposed to be admirable. Only a truly cultured person was believed to be capable of reacting sentimentally and getting the highest pleasure from the tender and the pathetic. This is shown by the following lines from Hannah More's poem, "Sensibility: An Epistle to the Honourable Mrs. Boscawen" (1787):

> Let not the vulgar read this pensive strain,
> Their jests the tender anguish would prophane.
> Yet these some deem the happiest of their kind,
> Whose low enjoyments never reached the mind.[13]

Burgoyne, too, in the preface to his comic opera, *Lord of the Manor* (1780), suggested that only the refined could be susceptible to the appeals of the sentimental drama with its scenes of tenderness and sensibility.

The term "sentimental" was quite fashionable in the eighteenth century. This is shown by the following passage (cited in *The New English Dictionary*) in Lady Bradshaigh's letter to Richardson in which she begged to be told the real meaning of the term: "Pray, sir, give me leave to ask you . . . what, in your opinion, is the meaning of the word *sentimental*, so much in vogue amongst the polite, both in town and country ?. . . Everything clever and agreeable is comprehended in that word. . . . I am frequently astonished to hear such a one is a *sentimental* man; we were a *sentimental* party; I have been taking a *sentimental* walk." Richardson's reply is not preserved, but he himself used the word in his novel *Sir Charles Grandison* (1754). Miss Harriet Byron, the heroine of this novel, wrote to Miss Lucy Selby: "And are there some situations in which a woman must conceal her true *sentiments* ? . . . Why was I born with a heart so open and sincere ?" The novel also contains the memorable words: "The French only are proud of their *sentiments* at this day; the English cannot bear them. Story, story, story, is what they hunt after, whether sense or nonsense, probable or improbable." One recalls here Dr. Johnson's familiar remark: "Why, Sir, if you were to read Richardson for the story, your patience would be so much fretted that you would hang yourself." "But," he significantly added, "You must read him for the sentiment and consider the story as only giving occasion to the sentiment."[14] Thus no suggestion of opprobrium attached to the eighteenth century use of "sentiment", and no hint of any undesirable lack of emotional control was associated with it.

The general opinion is that from 1660 for nearly a century it was an age of reason, satire and didacticism; that its literature was marked by coldness and want of feeling, being the product of intelligence, wit and fancy rather than of emotion, passion and imagination. Such rigid and oversimplified generalisations are best avoided, as they overlook the complexity of the age. It is true, of course, that many of the intellectuals of the period accepted the notion that truth is a product of reason or common sense, rather than of faith, difficult speculation or inspiration. Moreover, the intellectual triumphs of Newton and Boyle had been produced by reason as a measuring rod of the real world. But at the same time the eighteenth century was, by contrast with the Restoration period, an age of enthusiasm, emotion and sentiment. Indeed, sentiment had become an important literary force long before Sterne wrote his *Sentimental Journey* (1768); and Henery Mackenzie, his *Man of Feeling* (1771). It is true that certain sections of contemporary society gave preference to rational thought and intellectual sophistication, to the elegance of manners and the erfinement of urban civilization. But there was at the same time a strong reaction against the sophistication and artificiality of high life, against the rationalism, scepticism and materialism of the "Enlightenment" civilization.

The sentimental comedy is regarded as the earliest artistic expression of reaction against this dry rationalism and materialism. But the doctrine of sovereign reason came to be obscured by floods of sentiment in other forms of literature as well. The new elements of middle-class ethos entered into the psychological and literary atmosphere of the classical age. The literary pair of Addison and Steele catered to a definitely middle-class taste which had ever been scandalized by the sceptical materialism and the free behaviour of the aristocracy. The pages of *The Tatler* and *The Spectator* breathe with a moralizing sentiment which was calculated to lead the public back to the simple, emotional values. As educators of the middle classes, they achieved great success in their endeavour "to enliven morality with wit, and to temper wit with morality." In *Spectator* 10, Addison announced his moral and educational programme for the rising middle classes: ". . . I have resolved to refresh their memories from day to day, till I have recovered them out of that desperate state of vice and folly into which the age has fallen." In order to realize this aim, *The Spectator* covered many subjects, including the "pleasures of the imagination" in numbers 411 to 421 where Addison applied the ideas of Locke to develop a theory of beauty in both art and nature.

Instinct with a middle-class spirit, the essays of Steele are particularly remarkable for their sentimental interpretation of life and for reproving social vices and follies in touching appeals to virtue. For example, careless husbands and wives are sought to be reformed through remarkably tender descriptions of conjugal happiness (*Tatler* Nos. 85, 149 and 150). Besides he wrote some extremely sentimental short narratives. Referring to the sad tale of domestic life in *Tatler* 114, a correspondent wrote appreciatively in *Tatler* 118: "I have perused your *Tatler* of this day, and have wept over it with great pleasure; I wish you would be more frequent in your family pieces. . . ." Most of his tales[15] are as moving as domestic tragedies of Rowe and Lillo. By showing virtuous persons in distress, Steele's tales introduced sentimental literature to public much larger than the play-house audiences. It was almost a century later that Wordsworth presented in his *Lyrical Ballads* (1798) deeply moving tales of Woe, and characters as objects of sympathy and humanitarian feeling. One could say of Steele's tales, as Wordsworth said of his poems, that "the feeling therein developed gives importance to the action and situation, and not the action and situation to the feeling." It is the feeling that matters most in both cases. Steele, thus, revealed to his generation the sweet charm of tender sentiments, of family affections, and of the simple joys of the heart.

While Addison and Steele, through their moral and sentimental essays, widely influenced the rising middle classes, Anthony Ashley Cooper, third Earl of Shaftesbury, gained the attention of the aristocratic classes yet untouched by sentimentalism. His sentimental philosophy imparted considerable strength to the rising sentimental drama. According to him, man has natural goodness; he is endowed with moral sense which enables him to distinguish between right and wrong, and to prefer the right. It is natural for him to feel sympathy and love for his fellowmen, to be prompted by an instinctive pity for their misfortunes. Instinctively he finds virtue beautiful and is drawn towards it by a natural attraction, unless he happens to be depraved by a wrong kind of education. What normally impels him to lead a virtuous life is the attractive beauty of virtue itself. He finds his highest happiness in exercising his natural instincts of pity, love and benevolence. However, one becomes miserable "by having self-passions too intense or strong."[16] Hence the need for educating the instincts, training the feelings and cultivating good taste. In this way man can pursue with a "disinterested" affection what his moral sense, when allowed to develop naturally, recognises as right.

According to Shaftesbury, man is instinctively prompted to act virtuously by his natural affections, and in their exercise he finds his greatest happiness. He does not deny the existence in man of the self-regarding instincts, and even of those instincts which are not "tending either to any good of the public or private."[17] But he emphasizes that while anti-social passions like malice and misanthropy are not natural to man, his benevolent and altruistic emotions are innate. The human heart is as good and beautiful as the spirit of Nature that binds all things in natural co-ordination, in peace and lovelinesss. He believes in the divine perfection of Nature, that is, the whole order of God's creation. This brings to mind what Addison says in *Spectator* No. 393: "... Providence has imprinted so many Smiles on Nature, that it is impossible for a Mind which is not sunk in more gross and Sensual Delights to take a survey of them without several secret Sensations of Pleasure." This perception of universal harmony, proportion and goodness in all nature gave a great fillip to ethical nature poetry. Many poets in the middle decades of the century such as Thomson, Akenside, Henry Needler, John Gilbert Cooper and James Harris responded to the appeal of Shaftesbury's benevolism and his belief in the perfection of Nature. The extent of this indebtedness has been commented upon at length in a valuable article by Moore.[18]

This school of sentimental philosophy was an incitement to humanitarian action and it had a humanizing effect on society. It challenged the callousness of the Church which "defended all inequalities as part of a divine dispensation."[19] One may perhaps trace the great increase in philanthropic activity in this age to the impulse given by Shaftesbury's theories: "A keener sensitiveness to the needs and sufferings of others, particularly of the poor, was not only reflected in literature but was seen in the lives of philanthropists and in the successive activities of the age—the foundation first of Charity Schools; then of Hospitals; and, in the last year of the century, of Sunday Schools. . . ."[20] Shaftesbury's system itself was largely the assimilation of ideas of the seventeenth century divines of the Latitudinarian school, who had preached to their congregations the ethics of benevolence, good nature, and tender, sentimental feeling. Their teachings encouraged the eigtheenth century cult of sensibility, with its exaltation of the man of feeling and its emphasis on the cultivation of emotions as the highest aim of education.

With many citations from the Latitudinarians R.S. Crane has shown[21] that there was a definite strain of anti-stoicism in their ethical and psychological teachings. He does not minimize Shaftesbury's influence in the preparation for sentimentalism but shows how the earliest impulse leading to its popular triumph in the eighteenth century is to be sought in the influence of these divines due to their propaganda of benevolence and tender feeling during the period from about 1660 to 1725. Struggling against the stoic stress on insensibility, these preachers disseminated a creed of sensibility, and asserted that far from suppressing the tender emotions "we ought rather to look upon them as the marks which distinguished men of genuine goodness from those who are merely righteous or just."[22] These Latitudinarians put special emphasis on the emotional satisfaction and keen pleasure that man being naturally benevolent, obtained by commiserating with the wretched and helping them. Later Shaftesbury laid a similar emphasis on the reality of the altruistic instincts in man and on the pleasure to be obtained from compassionate feelings and acts of benevolence.

Shaftesbury combated the influence of the school of thought led by Thomas Hobbes, which had asserted that our natural passions "carry us to Partiality, Pride, Revenge, and the like."[23] But in the middle of the seventeenth century the mechanism of Hobbes had been opposed by a group of philosophers who came to be known as the Cambridge Platonists.[24] The chief members of this group were Cudworth, Henry More and John Smith. They had found that Hobbes's philosophy denied the possibility of moral and spiritual experiences which they found real and important. Shaftesbury also detested Hobbes's doctrines which turned morality into mere expediency and which undermined the artistic impulses and achievement of mankind. Later on, Rousseau, the author of *Emile* (1762), preached a natural and simple life. He recommended faith in mankind and in the ability to display sensibility and to shed tears. According to Rousseau, the laws of politeness were to be found in a benevolent heart. He advocated the teaching of benevolence, and happily spoke about his Emile: "The good he does comes from his heart, not his purse. He gives the wretched his time, his care, his affection, himself. . . ." Rousseau's protests against the Enlightenment civilization and his ideas about the natural man reinforced the popular doctrines of the Shaftesbury school. He thus gave further impetus to the rise of the whole sentimental movement in thought which was the manifestation of the psychological need of the age in an atmosphere of emotional starvation.

According to Shaftesburian philosophy, then, nature as a whole is beneficent; man is by nature inclined to good, not evil; it is the society which corrupts his instinctive preference for truth, beauty and goodness. These ideas which attained wide popularity furnished a philosophical basis for a new emphasis on feeling, natural dignity and simple virtue—the values that constituted the nucleus of sentimentalism. Consequently, much of the literature of the age idealized the simple, honest man with a kind heart. Mark Akenside's *Pleasures of the Imagination* (1746) presented a sentimental kind of aesthetics. In *The Seasons* (1726-30) Thomson who called Shaftesbury the friend of Man celebrated with an intensity of feeling the charm of the English countryside. Collins, Cooper, Joseph Warton and Gray disseminated various tenets of the sentimental faith—the beauty of tender melancholy, the moral power of natural beauty, the innocence of the state of nature, the superiority of emotion to intellect and the inhumanity of cruelty towards God's creation.

The major novelists of the period advocated the cultivation of a feeling heart. In the eighteenth century tears were regarded as a definite symptom of such a heart. A person of sentiment or sensibility would take every opportunity to burst into a flood of tears as they were deemed to be sanctifying. The cult of distress was indeed an important aspect of the cult of sensibility. The eminent writers of the age used such significant expressions as "Never before have I revelled in such luxury of tears"; "pity the greatest luxury the soul of sensibility is capable of relishing"; "voluptuousness of sorrow"; and "a pleasing kind of distress."[25] Sir Richard Steele, in the epilogue to his play, *The Lying Lover* (1703), wrote that to excite mirth was a lower achievement than "with pity to chastise delight." In *Tatler* No. 89 he spoke about "that calm and elegant satisfaction which the vulgar call melancholy" but which "is the true and proper delight of men of knowledge and virtue." In the preface to *The Conscious Lovers* (1722) he spoke of a "joy too exquisite for laughter." With many writers of the age, pathos became a highly desirable element, and they tried to evoke from their readers a sentimental response which was characterised by an element of enjoyment as well as of grief or pity. According to Sir Leslie Stephen, such a response is the name of "the mood in which we make a luxury of grief."[26]

Sentimentalism became in the eighteenth century part of a larger process by which life and literature were being made more human and humane. There was an increasing realization of the hardships which the majority of mankind had to suffer. This could be seen in men's changing attitude towards one another. In France, the effects could be seen in the decline of religious fanaticism. The Huguenots who had survived Louis XIV's terrible persecutions in the seventeenth century France were now treated with understanding and sympathy. Voltaire exposed the cruelty of criminal trials with the result that torture and mutilation became rare. In Prussia, refugees from religious persecution in other countries were made welcome by its rulers like Frederick William I and his famous son, Frederick the Great. In England, Roman Catholics and Protestant Dissenters who had earlier suffered most annoying civil disabilities could now lead relatively peaceful lives.

The principal leaders of the Methodist movement opposed the apathy of the church of England that prevailed in the early part of the eighteenth century. Whereas previously petty crimes against property were punishable by death, juries now often refused to convict the accused criminals. The educators inveighed against callous teachers, and benevolent citizens donated money to foundling hospitals. Henry Fielding praised in *The Champion* (February 16, 1740) the vogue of charity; and in *Covent-Garden Journal* (May 5, 1752), he mentioned a very large number of schemes for helping the poor. Dr. Johnson, in *The Idler* (May 6, 1758), wrote that whenever people in general were asked to help in a good cause, they were ready to contribute something. Goldsmith's Chinese sage in *The Citizen of the World* (1762) spoke of England's exalted virtue in the cause of charity. The French social critic Abbe' de Saint-Pierre described this new spirit as "bienfaisance", while Fielding called it goodness of heart.

Many writers of the age laid emphasis on the cultivation of the feelings as though in sentiment, pity and tears they recognized the most effective teachers. The capacity to feel became the supreme test of character. For example, Richardson's perfect man, Sir Charles Grandison, is so framed that he is bound to pity and suffer. Clarissa, the heroine of *Clarissa Harlowe*, believes in a feeling heart even if it is attended with grief. Sterne, the author of *Tristram Shandy* and *A Sentimental Journey*, idealized feeling or sensibility, showing that sensibility alone made man generous, and enabled him to respond to the joys and sorrows of his fellow-creatures. These writers reflected the spirit of the contemporary sentimental movement. They placed accent on simple piety and natural feeling, on the "softest benevolence" and the "tenderest sentiments."

In view of this sentimentalism in life and literature,[27] it is misleading to call eighteenth century the age of reason or savage pessimism, or enlightened scepticism. It was no less an age of sentiment. Professor Wood thinks that this sentimentalism grew from the essential temper of the Augustan age. He points out that "the thought of the early eighteenth century was based on Reason, and sentimentalism is closely connected with rationalism. The doctrine of the essential goodness of mankind was the corollary of the Augustan belief that Reason was a gift granted impartially to all men by Nature, without distinction of class or nationality."[28]

NOTES

1. Dale Underwood, *Etherege and the Seventeenth Century Comedy of Manners* (New Haven, Conn., 1957), p. 7.
2. L.C. Knights, "Restoration Comedy: The Reality and the Myth," *Explorations* (London, 1946), p. 149.
3. G.M. Trevelyan, *English Social History* (London, 1962), p. 337.
4. John Loftis, *Comedy and Society from Congreve to Fielding* (Stanford, 1959).
5. Cited by J.W. Krutch, *Comedy and Conscience after the Restoration* (New York, 1924), p. 93.
6. Cited by Kenneth Muir, *The Comedy of Manners* (London, 1970), p. 16.
7. *Critical Essays of the Seventeenth Century*, ed. J.E. Spingarn, 3 vols. (Oxford, 1908-9), II, p. 263.
8. A.W. Ward, *A History of English Dramatic Literature*, 3 vols. (1875; rpt. New York, 1966), III, pp. 514-15.
9. Thomas H. Fujimura, *The Restoration Comedy of Wit* (Princeton, 1953), pp. 185-86.
10. Jean Gagan, "Congreve's Mirabell and the Ideal of the Gentleman," *PMLA*, 79 (1964), pp. 422-27.
11. For various dates of the eighteenth-century usage of "sentimental" and its derivatives, see B. Sprague Allen, "The Dates of Sentimental and Its Derivatives," *PMLA*, 48 (1933), pp. 303-07.
12. O. Elton, *A Survey of English Literature, 1730-1780*, 2 vols. (1928; rpt. London, 1959), I, p. 284. A Nicoll, *A History of Early Eighteenth Century Drama, 1700-1750* (Cambridge, 1925), discusses some comedies of this period in a section entitled "Comedies of Sensibility," while in *A History of Late Eighteenth Century Drama, 1750-1800* (Cambridge, 1927) he examines similar plays in a section entitled "Sentimental Comedy."
13. Cited by Arthur Sherbo, *English Sentimental Drama* (East Lansing, Mich., 1957), pp. 8-9.

14. J. Boswell, *Life of Johnson*, ed. G.B. Hill, 6 vols. (Oxford, 1887), II, p. 175.
15. See, for example, *Tatler* Nos. 94, 95, 114, 198; *Spectator* Nos. 190, 375.
16. Anthony Ashley Cooper, Earl of Shaftesbury, *Characteristics of Men, Manners, Opinions, Times*, 3 vols. (London, 1727), II. p. 243.
17. Ibid, II, pp. 163-69. Ernest Tuveson, "The Importance of Shaftesbury," *ELH*, 20 (December 1953), pp. 267-99, argues that a great portion of Shaftesbury's work is devoted to the study of evil in human nature.
18. C.A. Moore, "Shaftesbury and the Ethical Poets in England, 1700-1760," *PMLA*, 31 (1916).
19. Moore, *Shaftesbury and the Ethical Poets*, p. 321.
20. Trevelyan, p. 347.
21. R.S. Crane, "Suggestions Toward a Genealogy of the 'Man of Feeling', " *ELH*, 1 (1934), pp. 205-30.
22. Ibid., pp. 216-17.
23. Thomas Hobbes, *Leviathan* (Oxford, 1952), p. 128.
24. For the chief features of their philosophy, see R.L. Brett, *The Third Earl of Shaftesbury* (London, 1951), pp. 13-32.
25. Cited by J.M.S. Tompkins, *The Popular Novel in England* (London, 1932), p. 103.
26. Sir L. Stephen, *History of English Thought in the Eighteenth Century*, 3rd ed. (London, 1902), II, p. 436.
27. For a consideration of sentimentalism in eighteenth-century literature, see A. Friedman, "Aspects of Sentimentalism in Eighteenth Century Literature," *The Augustan Milieu: Essays Presented to Louis A. Landa*, ed. H.K. Miller, et. al. (Oxford, 1970), pp. 247-61.
28. F.T. Wood, "The Beginnings and Significance of Sentimental Comedy," *Anglia*, 55 (1931), p. 384.

2

Advent of Sentimental Comedy

The eighteenth century drama was as much influenced by the social and literary phenomenon of sentimentalism as by the movement to reform the morals and manners of the nation. It became both pure and sentimental. The recognition of this fact after this survey should prepare us for the great popularity of sentimental comedy of the age. Also, as some of the traits of sentimentalism have been suggested above, we can readily see the justification for calling this comedy sentimental. It is difficult to agree with Professor Loftis when he asserts[1] that there was no such thing as sentimental comedy but only sentimentalism in comedy. He can be answered by saying that it should be called sentimental comedy because it is the quality of sentimentalism that really differentiates it from the Restoration comedy.

It is, however, true that "sentimental" includes too many qualities to have a specific meaning. Critics have not been able to offer a clear and comprehensive definition of the term. Ward and Nettleton find the root of sentimental drama in pity.[2] Bernbaum finds it in a certain belief in the essential goodness of human nature which he calls "the mainspring of sentimentalism" and the fundamental assumption of the sentimental playwrights.[3] Nicoll seems to find its quality in pathos and in a moral problem. An adequate definition of sentimental comedy must cover these important points and perhaps even more in order to specify its distinguishing features. The difficulty with these definitions is that none of them is quite applicable to every sentimental comedy of the age. We may have ten sentimental comedies, each stressing different sentimental elements. So, instead of defining sentimental comedy, it may be more helpful to say that a play becomes sentimental if it emphasises one or more of the various sentimental elements, stated below.

It is not easy to suggest a satisfactory substitute for the term sentimental comedy while referring to such plays as *The Careless Husband*, *The Conscious Lovers*, *The Foundling* and *The West Indian*. Their principal appeal is not to the sense of the comic, but to more serious emotions. They substitute sentiment for laughter; they make their audience experience the gentler emotions and witness the triumph of virtue; they radiate a new sentimental and humanitarian zeal. It is difficult to admire the substitute "Exemplary Comedy", suggested by Mr. Smith.[4] This nomenclature gives no adequate idea of the most distinguishing feature of this comedy. It is, after all, its marked emphasis on the element of sentiment or sensibility that gives it its distinctive tone and mood.

Sentimental comedy endeavours to give tender and tearful joy instead of a comic denouement. Intent upon raising a sigh and calling forth a tear like many sentimental novels of the age, it leaves its audience rather with a warm glow than with a laugh or smile. It contains a sympathetic, serious and emotional treatment of a serious subject, though it ends happily. Its action is often mixed with expressions of tremulous emotion and intense pathos. Its principal characters show remarkably tender minds and soft hearts and are at times on the verge of permanent distress. It has, therefore, been aptly termed sentimental comedy by such scholars as Ward, Waterhouse, Nettleton, Bernbaum, Krutch and Nicoll. Aptly because, it may be repeated, the humour of the early comedy gives place here to sentiment or feeling as the predominant element. The sentimental comedy appeals to the heart rather than intellect; it stresses human nature than social manners; it evokes pity for virtue in distress. Serious and didactic, it consciously expresses a moral precept. Professor Wood rightly observes that "as morality enters in to any marked degree, intellect must yield up its place to sentiment, and we immediately begin to move away from the comic spirit."[5]

Reacting against the bawdy and inhuman comedy of manners, the sentimental playwrights made a clear profession of writing with a definite moral purpose. They often appealed to their patrons to note that their comedies complied with the new ideas of stage morality. Cibber, for example, proclaimed that his *Careless Husband* (1704) was written in answer to the best critics who "have long and justly complain'd that the coarseness of most characters in our late comedies have been unfit entertainments for people of quality, especially the ladies." It was Steele, however, who was foremost theoretical advocate of this moral, sentimental comedy. He actively campaigned for this new drama. In *Tatler* No. 3, he answered the author of *The Country Wife* because he "condescends to represent the insults done to the honour of the bed without just reproof." In *Tatler* No. 8 he referred to Ravenscroft's *The London Cuckolds* as a heap of vice and absurdity. In *Spectator* No. 51, he spoke of the smuttiness that marred so many dramatic compositions. He hit at the kind of play in which "a fine Gentleman . . . lies with half the women in the play, and is at last rewarded with her of the best character in it."

Steele suggested a new way of writing in which there was no place for the bawdy. In *Spectator* No. 65, Etherege's *The Man of Mode* was condemned as "a perfect contradiction of good manners, good sense, and common honesty." He wanted such plays "whence it is impossible to return without strong impressions of honour and humanity." In *Spectator* No. 525 he wrote that the writings of the Restoration period "are such as would tempt one to think there had been an association among the wits of those times to rally legitimacy out of our island," but as for himself, "I must confess it has been my ambition, in the course of my writings, to restore, as well as I was able, the proper ideas of things."

Sentimental comedy, as stated above, is based on sentiment or emotion rather than reason or intellect. It is thus different from the Restoration comedy which excluded sentiment, keeping emotional idealism well outside its sphere of hard realism. While Collier had protested only against the indecency of the Restoration comedy, Steele and others had also been shocked at its singularly inhuman spirit. Indeed, the Restoration writers, like Hobbes, had viewed emotion with dislike and contempt. Steele, however, strongly defended sentiment in the new comedy. In the preface to *The Lying Lover* (1702), speaking of his remorse-stricken hero, he wrote: "The Anguish He there expresses, and the mutual Sorrow between an only Child, and a tender Father in that Distress are, perhaps, an Injury to the Rules of Comedy; but I am sure they are a Justice to those of Morality." In the epilogue we are told that laughter is despicable, "a distorted passion"; while pity is of divine origin, and "made us ourselves both more approve and know." Pity is equated with benevolence and hailed as something which Nature gave "for man to man."

Such grave sentiments were expressed again and again by this most prominent practitioner of the sentimental comedy in the early eighteenth century. In *Tatler* No. 8. he voiced the hopes of sentimental dramatists: "What may not be brought to pass by seeing generous things performed before our eyes?" His ideals were satisfied by such serious comedies as Cibber's *Lady's Last Stake* and *The Careless Husband.* In *Tatler* No. 8, he worte: "The *grave* and *serious* performances of such as write in the most engaging manner by a kind of divine impulse, must be most effectual persuasives to goodness." "To be apt to shed tears," he wrote in *Tatler* No. 68, "is a sign of great as well as little spirit." Again, in *Tatler* No. 134, he pointed out that tenderness, compassion and humanity were, as much as reason, attributes which distinguished men from brutes. Steele, thus, keeps up a constant propaganda to influence public literary taste and to establish the sentimental tradition. He strengthened the theoretical basis of the moral, sentimental comedy by praising or blaming in his essays the current plays in accordance with his principles.

Advocated by Steele, favoured by the sentimental middle classes, and supported by a contemporary sentimental movement in thought that was encouraged by ethical theories assuming human benevolence, the sentimental comedy became a popular form of drama in the eighteenth century. Coming into existence even before the beginning of the century, it was the earliest expression of that sentimental view of life which, as shown above, found expression in several forms of the eighteenth century literature. "It was not, indeed, in the theatre," says Bateson, "but in the essays of Steele and Shaftesbury and the novels of Richardson and Sterne that 'sentimentalism' received its fullest and perfected expression."[6] But perhaps it is nearer the truth to say that it was in the theatre that sensibility found the largest scope. As we shall see below, every decade of the century saw the successful production of plays which portrayed characters whose joys and sorrows were productive of heart-stirring emotions, whose problems were treated without shocking decorum, and whose exemplary conduct contributed to the edification of souls. These also depicted certain erring characters who finally showed goodness hidden in the depths of their souls, thus revealing human nature as essentially good and generous.

The contemporary audiences seem to have been in no mood to forego pleasure that accrued from the shedding of gentle tears; they enjoyed the pathetic scenes in these comedies, and wept with their characters, thus exhibiting a becoming sympathy for their species. As Nicoll remarks, " 'sympathetic' tears and 'sentimental' tears were almost synonymous terms for the eighteenth century."[7] The "honest" tears which Tom Davies says the spectators shed at Cibber's *Love's Last Shift* were "sympathetic" tears and thus highly commendable. In the preface to *The Conscious Lovers,* Steele approvingly refers to a certain General who wept over the distresses of Indiana, the virtuous heroine of this play. Sentimentalism, thus, meant "the return of what we may call sympathy to the theatre; it restored to comedy the humanity which the Restoration had suppressed."[8]

We shall now see how in every decade of the century the playwrights wrote comedies containing sentimental elements, showing various degrees of sentimentalism in their treatment of themes and characters. *The London Stage* makes it plain that most of them were quite popular in their time. In the first decade, Farquhar wrote several such comedies. Richard Estcourt's comedy *The Fair Example* (1703)[9] has a significant title. The "fair example" is set by its virtuous heroine, Lucia, who remains steadfast in her fidelity to her wicked husband, though her heart "bleeds with tenderness and pity." The prologue declares that "Some mirth, some pity, would our action move."

Steele's *The Funeral* (1701), though written mainly in an amusing style, contains several sentimental elements. For example, Trusty, the honest steward of Lord Brumpton, sentimentalizes over the virtuous Lord Hardy, the disinherited son of his master: "Forgive me, my honoured master (*Weeps . . . and hugs him*). I've often carried you in these arms that grasp you; they were stronger then, but if I die tomorrow. you're worth five thousand pounds by my gift—'tis what I've got in the family, and I return it to you with thanks. But alas ! do I live to see you want it ?" Many sentimental comedies of the period are replete with such pathetic expressions. Lord Hardy, Lady Sharlot, and Trusty are the exemplary characters of the play. Through Sable, an undertaker, Steele seems to denounce "the wits who take the liberty to deride all things that are magnificent and solemn." Virtue is rewarded, and vice is duly exposed at the end. In the preface to the play Steele says that its "innocence" moved the Duke of Devonshire "to the humanity of expressing himself in its favour," *The Funeral* long remained a stock play.

It is *The Lying Lover* (1703) which is Steele's first real sentimental comedy. In the preface Steele remarks that the pathetic scenes have often been applauded on the stage. For him it is time to assail debauchery, not with ridicule, but by causing the public to tremble with horror at its grievous consequences. In the prologue he says that he wrote this play "with just regard to a reforming age." The Dedication to the Duke of Ormond further testifies to his distinct moral purpose. His intention, he says, is "to banish out of conversation all Entertainment which does not proceed from Simplicity of Mind, Good Nature, Friendship and Honour." The scene in which Young Bookwit is comforted by his weeping father (V, iii) is the most serious and sentimental portion of the play, as it deliberately appeals to pity instead of laughter. Steele complains that this play was "damn'd for its Piety." Its sentimentalized morality reminds one of Hazlitt's remark that Steele's plays are "rather homilies in dialogue." In view of the extremely serious nature of the last act of *The Lying Lover*, Dr. Ward sees in it "the first instance of Sentimental Comedy proper."[10]

Cibber's *The Careless Husband* (1704) is a conscious attempt at meeting the demands of the new comedy. The Dedication to John Duke of Argyle, decries coarseness and shows Cibber's anxiety to reform contemporary comedy. Cibber writes that he "was long in hopes, that some able pen . . . would generously attempt to reform the town into a better taste, than the world generally allows 'em"; but, as that did not happen, he himself struck the first blow. Carried by the current of sentiment and morality, he treats his patrons to a moralizing, sentimental comedy. It is dominated throughout by its sentimental heroine, Lady Easy, who undergoes much suffering because of her erring husband. There is a sentimental scene (V, v) in which he repents and reforms, and is forgiven by his wife who weeps with joy. Sensibility colours the whole piece and determines both the characters and their actions. The play was a great success and took its place among favourites in the standard repertory of the theatre.

During the next five years, four comedies produced with distinct success are of the sentimental type. These are Mrs. Centlivre's *The Gamester* (1704), Steele's *The Tender Husband* (1705), Farquhar's *Beaux' Stratagem* ((1706), and Cibber's *The Lady's Last Stake* (1707). *The Gamester* attacks the vices of the gaming table. When Valere loses Angelica's gift, he is filled with remorse. Angelica breaks her engagement with him, but his humility acquired in his adversity causes her heart to beat as if "the strings were breaking." After his reformation, she forgives and marries him. The last two acts contain many serious passages. There is, thus, a good deal of sentimentalism in this comedy. *The Beaux' Stratagem*, though mainly a gay comedy, contains several sentimental elements.

The Tender Husband which Bateson calls Steele's dramatic masterpiece might look unsentimental when placed beside *The Lying Lover*. But it is not altogether without sentimental touches. Steele's Dedication to Addison declares that he took care "to avoid everything that might look Ill-natur'd, Immoral, or prejudicial to what the Better Part of Mankind hold Sacred and Honourable." In this play Clerimont Senior succeeds in making his too free a wife realize the error of her ways. There is a sentimental scene (V, i) in which she kneels, weeps, and is forgiven. The moral is that happiness between man and wife can be established only on the basis of love. Such an emphasis on domestic virtues shows a genuine intrusion of the middle-class values into the drama of the age.

The Lady's Last Stake is quite a sentimental comedy. Bernbaum rightly says that "the general trend and the denouement of both (its) plots are exceptionally serious." Cibber declares in the Dedication that "A Play, without a just Moral, is a poor and trivial Undertaking; and 'tis from the Success of such Pieces, that Mr. *Collier* was furnish'd with an advantageous Pretence of laying his unmerciful axe to the Root of the Stage." In this play, Cibber exposes the evil of gambling in its most hideous form. All the erring characters finally repent and reform, thanks to Sir Friendly Moral who has great belief in the goodness of human nature. There are many long passages of emotional speech, especially in the last Act. In view of its conspicuous sentimentalism, Professor Wood says, "If *The Tender Husband* marked a retrogression in the march of sentimentalism, *The Lady's Last Stake* represented a decided advance."[11] The play remained a favourite through the first half of the century, and was performed as late as 1786.

Charles Shadwell's comedy, *The Fair Quaker of Deal* (1709) is sentimental as its lead characters undergo reformation, and its last scene gives importance to benevolence and forgiveness. The play was a great success.

Even Addison, the author of the neo-classic tragedy, *Cato* (1713), found himself persuaded by Steele to write a sentimental comedy, *The Drummer*, or *The Haunted House* (1715). It has a pathetic character, Lady Truman, who believes her husband to be dead and sincerely mourns him. Addison, thus, violated one of the principles of classic drama that a comedy should be a comedy from first to last, that it is not to allow any pathetic element to enter into its composition. Addison's purpose is stated in the epilogue: "No man need blush though true to marriage-vows, / Nor be a jest though he should love his spouse." If the response of the Drury Lane audience to this comedy was discouraging, it was only because its plot lacked novelty, and not because it was sentimental. Steele, however, hoped that "the reader will see many beauties that escaped the audience; the touches being too delicate for every taste in a popular assembly."

Charles Johnson wrote a sentimental comedy, *The Masquerade* (1718), in imitation of Cibber's *The Lady's Last Stake*. Its principal character, Lady Frances Ombre, is addicted to gambling like Cibber's Lady Gentle. She is saved from ruin and brought to repentance by her devoted husband. As the play lacked originality, it was a failure. The year 1720, however, saw a much better sentimental comedy in Charles Shadwell's *The Irish Hospitality*. Its central character, Sir Patrick Worthy, is a perfect embodiment of Shaftesburian benevolism. "I think myself an earthly steward," says he, "deputed by Heaven to distribute that fortune it has entrusted me with, on my fellow creatures." In many sentimental comedies of the age there are benevolent characters who express similar sentiments and philosophize about moral and social ideals.

Steele's another successful play, *The Conscious Lovers* (1722), is one of the most distinguishing examples of sentimental comedy. The title itself sugggests sentimentalism, as "conscious" means "conscientious." Its main interest is sentimental as there is much of pathos and moralizing. In the preface Steele proclaims that its chief intention is to be an "innocent Performance." He is glad to inform the reader that the distresses of the heroine, Indiana, drew tears from a General. Parson Adams in Fielding's *Joseph Andrews* owns that this play has some things "almost solemn enough for a sermon." *The Conscious Lovers,* thus, makes a clear departure from the Restoration tradition. It was so popular in its time that it ran for twenty-eight consecutive nights. This extraordinary success meant a considerable triumph for sentimentalism. Kies has shown[12] that the German dramatist, Lessing, was influenced by Steele, and that *The Conscious Lovers* was the specific model of Lessing's two sentimental comedies, *Der Freigeist* (1749) and *Die Juden* (1749).

In 1728, Cibber completed an unfinished manuscript of Vanbrugh's play, *A Journey to London*, but changed the title of the produced version to *The Provok'd Husband* (1727). Always alive to the currents of the public taste, Cibber recast the original play from a sentimental stand-point. He writes in the preface that Vanbrugh intended the provoked husband to turn his frivolous wife out of doors. Cibber, however, found this too severe for comedy and, therefore, preserved the lady's chastity to facilitate reconciliation between the husband and wife. The play is given a happy ending through the sentimental device of repentance and reform. Probably, Vanbrugh never contemplated the reformation of Lady Townly as in Cibber. Cibber also cut out the bawdy from the original fragment in keeping with the current trend towards a moral comedy. This sentimental comedy was so popular that it had an initial run of twenty-eight nights and remained a stock play for nearly a century.

Even Henry Fielding who, as a dramatist, is better known for his literary and political burlesques such as *Tom Thumb* (1730), *Pasquin* (1735), and *The Historical Register* (1736), did not remain unaffected by the vogue for sentiment. Bernbaum brings out the sentimental elements of *The Modern Husband* (1731) in order to show that Fielding did not devote himself to true comedy consistently. The Licensing Act of 1737, however, made him abandon the stage and write novels which themselves were not free from sentimentality, though he avowedly disapproved of Richardson's sentimentalism.

It is rather curious that the sentimental comedy fell into a decline during the fourth and fifth decades, though the temper of the age was quite favourable to its advancement. In fact, sentimentalism had become by this time a strong force and appeared prominently in the poetry and the novel. One reason for the decline of sentimental comedy may be the poverty of any persuasive English dramatic criticism after the death of Steele, the greatest theoretical advocate of sentimental comedy. Another could be the Licensing Act which accounted for a general decline in drama by driving potential playwrights out of the theatre. During this period, the French *comedie larmoyante* was definitely superior to the English sentimental comedy, though these two schools of comedy arose out of similar influences. As shown by Bernbaum (Chapter 10), the English sentimental comedies before 1750 did not display the easy assurance of manner and refinement of feeling possessed by the plays of De la Chaussee, Marivaux, Voltaire and Gresset. The French dramatists obtained new effects from familiar themes, bringing out the emotional values more convincingly. Their sentimental comedies were often adapted by the English writers after 1750.

In England, sentimental comedy did not, however, disappear altogether during this period. Besides minor sentimental comedies such as Popple's *The Lady's Revenge* (1733),

Jacob's *The Prodigal Reformed* (1737), James Dance's *Pamela* (1741), there were three of real merit. These were John Kelly's *The Married Philosopher* (1732), Benjamin Hoadly's *The Suspicious Husband* (1747), and Edward Moore's *The Foundling* (1748). Bernbaum shows that Kelly's play, an adaptation of Destouches' *Le Philosophe Marie* (1727), omits many sentimental lines and passages in the original, and it lacks the delicacy with which the French dramatists of the age generally described the sentimental emotions. Hoadly's sentimental comedy deals with Strictland, the suspicious husband of a young wife, though it eschews bawdry. It remained immensely popular for a long time. In the prologue to *The Foundling*, Henry Brooke states the sentimental aim of the author:

He rather aims to draw the melting sigh,
Or steal the pitying tear from Beauty's eye,
To touch the strings that humanize our kind,
Man's sweetest strain, the music of the mind.

The scene in which the virtuous Fidelia, supposed to be a foundling, is restored to her parents, is thoroughly sentimental. This play is the culmination of the sentimental comedies of the early eighteenth century. Nicoll looks upon it "as the connecting link between the sentimentalism of the early and the sentimentalism of the late eighteenth century."[13] The play met with great success at its first performance. It was, however, criticised for its vulgar fop, Faddle, in the March number of the *Gentleman's Magazine* for 1748.

The sentimental comedy, thus, suited the popular taste of the age in the early eighteenth century. It may be added that the type of tragic drama which provided real emotional sustenance to this age was also pathetic and sentimental. In the early years of the Restoration period the heroic play, often tragic, was very popular because it met the special needs of a decadent aristocracy. The chief emotion it aroused was not pity or terror, but admiration, that is, teaching through example, that was admired and imitated. But as the century drew to a close, it faded, yielding place to pathetic tragedy, as the latter alone, with its emphasis on pity, could satisfy the new demands of a changing society for sentiment instead of heroic action. Thomas Otway's *The Orphan* (1680) and *Venice Preserved* (1682), and Thomas Southerne's *The Fatal Marriage* (1694) and *Oroonoko* (1695) are tragedies based upon pity. Each puts emphasis on a pathetic woman who is a victim of circumstances for which she is not responsible and over which she seems to have no control. This is clear from what happens to Monimia in *The Orphan*, Belvidera in *Venice Preserved*, Isabella in *The Fatal Marriage*, and Imoinda in *Oroonoko*. As this type of tragedy appeals to pity, Professor Nettleton remarks, "Perhaps the real origin of sentimental comedy should be sought not simply in the moralized comedy of Cibber but in the somewhat sentimentalized tragedy of Otway and Southerne."[14]

Nahum Tate took many liberties with the Shakespearean drama in the name of pity. Today we may ridicule him for distorting *King Lear*, but Dr. Johnson spoke for a whole century when he expressed his gratitude to him. Sentimental tragedy was the only acceptable type of tragedy in the eighteenth century. Colley Cibber in this prologue to *Perolla and Izodora* (1705) thought it necessary to apologize for having "neglected too, tho' much in Fashion,/To murther Innocence to move Compassion." Rowe's *The Fair Penitent* (1703), a domestic tragedy, is "a melancholy Tale of private Woes." The opening lines of the prologue are significant:

> Long has the fate of kings and empires been
> The common business of the tragic scene,
> As if the misfortune made the throne her seat,
> And none could be unhappy but the great.

In the Dedication to the Duchess of Ormond, Rowe comments that distress and misfortunes are among the main designs of tragedy and that "to excite this generous pity" is a sign of success in the dramatist. The popular success of this sentimental tragedy encouraged its author to write a similar play, *Jane Shore* (1713). The prologue says that it is about "A tale which, told long since in homely wise,/Hath never failed of melting gentle eyes." Dr. Johnson, in his *Life of Rowe*, testifies to the popularity of *Jane Shore*: "This play, consisting chiefly of domestic scenes and private distress, lays hold upon the heart. . . This, therefore, is one of those pieces which we still welcome on the stage." He particularly liked[15] the heroine's last moving appeal, "Forgive me:—but forgive me," as she dies in her husband's arms.

The popularity of Rowe's sentimental tragedies and Steele's pathetic tales appears to have encouraged Aaron Hill to write a domestic tragedy, *The Fatal Extravagance* (1721). The following lines of its prologue bring to mind those of *The Fair Penitent*:

> Empires o'erturned, and heroes held in chains,
> Alarm the mind but give the heart no pains.
> To ills remote from our domestic fears,
> We lend our wonder, but withhold our tears.

This moral, sentimental tragedy was quite popular in its time and was later borrowed from by Edward Moore for his well-known domestic tragedy, *The Gamester* (1753). Even more popular was Lillo's sentimental, domestic tragedy, *The London Merchant* (1731). Instead of dealing with the fall of an illustrious person, Lillo portrays George Barnwell, a merchant's clerk, as being led astray by a heartless courtesan to rob his employer and murder his uncle. He is sincerely penitent before being brought to execution. The play attained enduring recognition; it was translated into French, German and Dutch. In the preface to the translation into German of *Thomson's Tragedies* (1756), Lessing expressed his preference for *The London Merchant* over Addison's *Cato*, because the former was a more moving one.

The preference in this period for plays that slighted the neo-classical rules of decorum and the three unities, is significant. It shows that the eighteenth century dramatists did not desist from taking such liberties as were in accord with the national temperament. And this would have happened even if Dryden, the liberal classicist, had not paid a spontaneous homage to Shakespeare and put forward, in his *Essay of*

Dramatic Poesy, a defence of the irregular Elizabethan drama as opposed to the regular classical French drama. These pathetic tragedies pleased the beholders with sentiments of pity and compassion. In these popular sentimental tragedies and comedies of the period, the emphasis was on sympathy and pity and emotion. The contemporary audiences enjoyed weeping for the virtuous character as victim: they took great pleasure in showing benevolence in pitying another man's distress.[16]

The sentimental comedy was also popular during the latter half of the century, though Nicoll perhaps exaggerates when he remarks that "the whole of the dramatic literature of this time is influenced directly or indirectly, by sentimentalism."[17] In the sixth decade of the century hardly any really good sentimental comedies appeared. While the atmosphere was quite favourable to the progress of the genre, it just happened that no playwright of the calibre of Cibber or Steele tried his hand during this period at the sentimental comedy, perhaps because the novel was thought to satisfy much better the emotional needs of the time. Playwrights like Foote and Colman tried at times to ridicule the excesses of sentiment in the drama, but they also thought it expedient at times to surrender to the popular taste for anything of emotional appeal. For example, Foote's *The Minor* (1760) is full of sentimental motives and actions; and Colman who had attacked sentimentalism in *Folly Honeycomb* (1760) and written *The Jealous Wife* (1761) in the old comic tradition, introduced sentimental elements in his best play in order to keep in touch with the current fashion. *The Clandestine Marriage* (1766) which he wrote in collaboration with that expert judge of the current mood, David Garrick, sought to give pleasure "reaped from the tender emotions of the heart." Despite its comic portions, it is, as Bernbaum shows, sentimental in its main plot and principal characters.[18] Speaking of Fanny in this play, Elizabeth P. Stein says that her "excess of sensibility, because it forces itself continuously upon our attention, becomes ridiculous."[19] But it is precisely this excess of emotionalism or sensibility which is an important feature of the sentimental comedy. Such an excess of sensibility, delicacy or refinement does not seem to have appeared ridiculous to the contemporary audiences. *The Clandestine Marriage* was a tremendous and lasting success. This seems to have induced Colman to write another comedy, *The English Merchant* (1767), which is conspicuously sentimental. It is based on, though inferior to Voltaire's sentimental comedy, *L'Ecossaise* (1760). In Colman's play, a character describes the meeting between father and daughter in these words: "First they wept for grief; then they wept for joy; and then they wept for grief again (IV)." Interestingly, the drama critic for the March number of the *Gentleman's Magazine* (1767), chose this feature of the play for comment, speaking of "a luxury in tears that laughter can never taste." The play was moderately successful and revived occasionally.

There are many sentimental comedies, some containing both pathetic and comic elements, written during and after the seventh decade of the century. It will be tedious and unnecessary to discuss at length their sentimental elements. What is important for our purposes is the extent of the immediate, even subsequent, popularity of such sentimental comedies as are of a less alloyed or mixed character.

William Whitehead's *The School for Lovers* (1762), an adaptation of Fontenelle's *Le Testament*, is one of the outstanding sentimental comedies of the period. According to Bernbaum, it inaugurates the revival of sentimental comedy. The dramatist's sentimental aim is stated in the prologue:

> Plain comedy to-night, with strokes refined,
> Would catch the coyest features of the mind,
> Would play politely with your hopes and fears,
> And sometimes similes provoke, and sometimes tears.

He distrusted laughter, because "That eager zeal to laugh the vice away/May hurt some virtue's intermingling ray." He, therefore, dwells upon the depiction of distress and emotions. The play was favourably reviewed by Dr. John Hawkesworth, the dramatic critic for the *Gentleman's Magazine*. He described its sentiments as chaste and elegant, and some of its situations as "touching and tender in the highest degree." *The London Magazine* referred to its plot as full of "delicacy and sentiment."[20] This play had a good run of thirteen nights in its first season and was a steady success for several seasons.

Mrs. Frances Sheridan's *The Discovery* (1763) depicts a son sacrificing his love to save his father from ruin. Some of its scenes (IV, i and ii, for example) approximate to those of the French *comedie larmoyante.* This sentimental comedy was a considerable success in its first season, achieving seventeen performances. Isaac Bickerstaff's *The Maid of the Mill* (1765) is a dramatization of Richardson's sentimental *Pamela,* with Mr. B. converted into Lord Aimworth, a model of propriety. This sentimental piece was so successful that it achieved twenty-nine performances in the first season, and was revived frequently throughout the period. In Mrs. Elizabeth Griffith's *The Double Mistake* (1766) the sentimental heroine, Emily, is presented as an innocent sufferer. Bernbaum calls attention to the artistic blemishes of the play and concludes that its success "shows how completely sentimentalism had for the time being recaptured the theatrical public." According to *The London Stage,* however, this play ran a few nights in its first month, and was not r evived.

Mrs. Elizabeth Griffith's *The School for Rakes* (1769) portrays the innocent heroine, Harriot, whose sufferings are calculated to melt the hearts of the tender and sensible. The prologue, s poken by Mr. King, speaks of tears as well as laughter: "Sigh when you laugh, and laugh whene'er you cry." Dr. John Hawkesworth, in his review of the play in the *Monthly Review,* remarked: "This piece is not much calculated to excite laughter but it produces higher pleasure than laughter can give." The play ran well for a year and then achieved two performances.

The popular sentimental comedies of Hugh Kelly and Richard Cumberland merit special mention. Though Kelly was critical of "the extremes of sentimental gloom," he himself wrote plays cast in the sentimental mode. Dibdin, historian of the stage, thought it necessary to criticise him for taking advantage of "the rage that then prevailed for sentiment."[21] But this remark might as well have been directed to many other dramatists of the age. In the preface to his sentimental comedy, *The School for Wives* (1773), Kelly supports the sentimental school of dramatic composition. Speaking of himself in the third person he says that "he has some laugh, yet he hopes he has also some lesson; and fashionable as it has been lately for the wits . . . to ridicule the Comic Muse, when a little grave, he must think that she degenerates into farce, where the grand business of instruction is neglected." The play deals with the reclamation of a prodigal husband, Mr. Belville, and shows in Mr. Torrington a benevolent figure who has a strong faith in the goodness of human nature. The play enjoyed great success.

Kelly's earlier play, *False Delicacy* (1768), written in rivalry to Goldsmith's unsentimental play, *The Good-Natur'd Man*, is serious in tone. It is characterized by didactic moralizing dear to sentimental comedy. Though its characters, Lady Betty and Miss Marchmont, carry sentimental delicacy to false extremes, it cannot be denied that the appeal of the dramatist is to sentimental emotion. Kelly was shrewd enough to know that it paid to strike the popular chords of sentiment. The play was a tremendous success, "vociferously applauded by spectators and avidly read at home."

Bernbaum says that sentimental comedy suffered attack in the period 1768-72. But this did no real damage to the genre. This is shown by the popularity of Richard Cumberland's comedies, *The Brother* (1769) and *The West Indian* (1771). In its sentimental theme *The Brothers* is similar to Mrs. Griffith's *The School for Rakes*. It deals with the sufferings of the virtuous wife, Violetta, deserted by her husband, the elder Belfield. She is finally reunited to him as he repents his folly and reforms. The immediate success of *The Brothers* was great, and it was revived several times. Its success, however, was far surpassed by that of *The West Indian* which has been called the "culmination of the sentimental epoch," and "the extreme examples of

English sentimental comedy."[22] It deals with the reformation of Belcour and the distresses of Captain Dudley and his virtuous daughter, Louisa, the heroine. The play was a smash hit. Mrs. H. Cowley's *The Runaway* (1776) is a sentimental comedy, exalting true love of George Hargrave for Emily and showing their eventual triumph, made possible by Mr. Drummond, a middle-aged benevolist. Its great success showed that sentimental comedy continued to be as popular as before. Mrs. Elizabeth Griffith's *The Times* (1779) contains substantial elements of sensibility. Bedford engaged to be married to Sir William Woodley's niece is generous enough to withdraw his suit, knowing that the girl's affections are placed elsewhere. The play also deals with the reformation of Sir William's married nephew, Woodley. *The Town and Country* critic found *The Times* altogether destitute of comic situations and "by far too sentimental for the stage." Despite this, the play was a moderate success.

Some writers have exaggerated the sentimentalism of the eighteenth-century comedy. De Witt Croissant, for example, says that sentimental comedy was dominant throughout the eighteenth century.[23] Kenneth Muir asserts that in the middle of the century "the new plays were all sentimental."[24] Another writer expresses the same view when he states that Goldsmith's *The Good-Natur'd Man* (1768) "did not begin to stem the tide of sentimental comedies then gushing across the English stage."[25] Such statements tend to suggest that there was a virtual disappearance of non-sentimental or laughing comedy in the age. The performance records now finally available in *The London Stage* show that both sentimental and non-sentimental comedies were mounted with varying success. This is also shown by Sherbo (Chapter 7) who, working from John Genest's *Some Account of the English Stage from the Restoration in 1660 to 1830* (1832), compares the runs and revivals of selected sentimental and non-sentimental plays of the period 1750-80. George Winchester Stone, Jr., in his introduction to Part 4 of *The London Stage*, shows that during the period 1747-76, "Manners" comedy, Shakespeare's comedies and Intrigue comedy also flourished along with the sentimental comedy. The productions of Gay, Fielding, Murphy, Colman, Foote, Goldsmith and Sheridan, show that laughing comedy was never really eclipsed by the sentimental comedy.

But although the sentimental comedy was not dominant throughout the eighteenth century, it was, as shown above, quite a popular form of drama in the age. From Sherbo's examination (Chapter 7) of the contemporary critical reaction to key plays in the sentimental canon (written between 1750 and 1780) in the four leading periodicals, we learn that the critics, by and large, praised the sentimentally conceived plays, though they were also conscious that comedies should excite laughter.

NOTES

1. Loftis, *Comedy and Society*, p. 127.
2. A.W. Ward, *English Dramatic Literature*, III, p. 495; G.H. Nettleton, *English Drama of the Restoration and Eighteenth Century* (New York, 1914), pp. 155, 266.
3. E. Bernbaum, *The Drama of Sensibility* (Boston, 1915), p. 2.
4. J.H. Smith, *The Gay Couple in Restoration Comedy* (Cambridge, Mass., 1948), p. 231. This term (as opposed to "sentimental") is again proposed by him in his article "Shadwell, the Ladies, and the Change in Comedy," *MP*, 46 (1948), pp. 22-33.
5. Op. cit., p. 369.
6. F.W. Bateson, *English Comic Drama, 1700-1750* (New York, 1963), p. 12.
7. A. Nicoll, *The Theory of Drama* (New York, 1931), p. 238.
8. Bateson, p. 7.
9. The dates are of the first performances, given in the play-lists in Nicoll, *Early Eighteenth Century Drama* and *Late Eighteenth Century Drama*.
10. Ward, *English Dramatic Literature*, III, p. 495.

11. Wood, p. 389.
12. Paul P. Kies, "Lessing's Relation to Early English Sentimental Comedy," *PMLA*, 47 (September 1932), pp. 807-26.
13. Nicoll, *Early Eighteenth Century Drama*, p. 207.
14 Nettleton, *English Drama of the Restoration and Eighteenth Century*, p. 155. He also makes this point in "The Drama and the Stage," *CHEL*, 10 (1912), p. 315.
15. G.B. Hill, ed., *Johnsonian Miscellanies* (Oxford, 1897), I, pp. 283-84.
16. This is well discussed by A.O. Aldridge, "The Pleasures of Pity," *ELH*, 16 (1949), pp. 76-87.
17. Nicoll, *Late Eighteenth Century Drama*, p. 124.
18. Bernbaum, p. 218. Some critics, however, believe that this play maintains the comic tradition. See, for example, Nettleton, *English Drama of the Restoration and Eighteenth Century*, pp. 257-63.
19. *David Garrick, Dramatist* (New York, 1938), p. 238.
20. Cited by Sherbo, p. 148.
21. Charles Dibdin, *A Complete History of the Stage* (London, 1795), V, p. 277.
22. Stanley Williams, "The English Sentimental Drama from Steele to Cumberland," *Sewanee Review*, 33 (1925), p. 406; an unidentified critic, cited in F.S. Boas, *An Introduction to Eighteenth-Century Drama* (Oxford, 1953), p. 305.
23. "Early Sentimental Comedy," *Essays on Dramatic Literature: The Parrott Presentation Volume*, ed. Hardin Craig (Princeton, 1935), pp. 51, 71.
24. *The Comedy of Manners*, p. 156.
25. R.J. Griffin, "Goldsmith's Augustanism: A Study of his Literary Works," unpub. diss., Univ. of California, Berkeley, 1965.

3

Nature of Sentimental Comedy

Sentimental comedy aimed at elevating human nature by depicting moral excellence. The assumption was that the spectators tended to imitate what they saw on the stage. This point was stressed by Steele in *Spectator* No. 446: "Whatever vices are represented upon the stage, they ought to be so marked and branded by the poet, as not to appear laudable nor amiable in the person who is tainted with them." In his *Short View*, Collier had lamented that the Restoration comedy not only represented vice but also rewarded it: "To what purpose is *Vice* thus preferred, thus ornamented, and carress'd, unless for imitation ?" Steele demanded that comedy must reward virtue and punish vice. In the sentimental comedy, virtue never goes unrewarded, and vice is always frustrated. It endeavours to elevate human nature by inspiring a desire for moral excellence. Its chief design is instruction rather than entertainment, and it employs poetic justice to fulfil this design. The pleasure, if any, arises from the spectacle of virtue finally triumphant. It attempts to show, as a rule, that the virtuous persons triumph over all obstacles, while the wicked are exposed at the end. The virtuous person may be a faithful lover or a wronged wife, or a lost child.

In *The Conscious Lovers,* it is the true lover Myrtle, and not the avaricious Cimberton, who is made to marry the virtuous Lucinda. In *The School for Lovers* it is the noble Lord Dorilant, not the unscrupulous Modely, who finally weds the virtuous Caelia. In *The Brothers* it is Belfield Jr., and not his villainous elder brother, who is rewarded at the end with the hand of Sophia. Whosoever seeks marriage for purely material gains is shown as badly failing in his designs. To the sentimentalist, as Gallaway points out, virtue is not only admirable, it is victorious."[1] The virtuous maidens like Indiana in *The Conscious Lovers,* Fidelia in *The Foundling* and Emily in *The Runaway,* though they have to suffer much, are finally rewarded and united with their true lovers in the midst of emotional speeches. In the sentimental comedy, no sacrifice is allowed to go unrewarded and it always receives payment in material currency. Such a consistent employment of poetic justice tends to reduce everything to a neat, but artificial and tiresome pattern. What Schorer says of Hugh Kelly applies to the sentimental playwrights in general: "An earthly reward for sweetness, tenderness, generosity, and moral excellence, and a reward that comes in terms of a substantial fortune is this sentimentalist's easiest and most damnable assumption."[2]

The themes of sentimental comedy arise from a general protest against unethical attitude towards literature and from sensitivity to changes in patterns of behaviour due to new ethical theories. Whereas the Restoration comedy mocks at the conventional moral code, the sentimental comedy upholds traditional values. Its themes and the treatment they receive read like protests against the immoral atmosphere of the plays of Etherege and Wycherley. Cuckoldry, inconstancy and jealousy are either abandoned or treated differently. Love and marriage are no longer treated flippantly, nor shown as incompatible. The themes of sentimental comedy are easily adapted for the introduction of emotional situations, lofty sentiments, tender expressions and moral teaching. It presents conventional virtue in a favourable light, puts its moral on emotional or sentimental basis, and contains the expression of noble thought. What is glorified is moral excellence rather than flippancy, sentiment rather than wit.

The sentimental comedy deals primarily with matters of private life, the problems of love, courtship and marriage. It emphasizes the sanctity of matrimony, discarding mere gallantry or sex-antagonism or love-chase. An erring husband or a wronged wife is not allowed to cause breakdown of marriage. The reconciliation of an estranged husband and wife is a prominent theme of this comedy. To give only one example, Sir Charles Easy in *The Careless Husband* wrongs his virtuous wife, Lady Easy, by carrying an intrigue with Lady Graveairs, and having an affair with his wife's maid, Mrs. Edging. The wronged wife knows all this, but does not upbraid him, fearing that the "uneasy thought of my continual jealousy may tease him to a fixed aversion."[3] In the climactic scene of the play, she has the mortification of discovering her husband and her maid, both asleep in two easy chairs in Sir Charles's room. In a Restoration comedy such a wronged wife might well have been provoked into seeking divorce or even committing adultery. But to Lady Easy, marriage seems to mean a certain commitment to an ideal; it is not something to be trifled with. Instead of reproaching her husband, she hastens to put her own steinkirk upon his head lest he should catch cold. Realizing his wife's considerateness and her long-suffering love, Sir Charles is shamed into turning over a new leaf. A little later, he tells Lady Graveairs that in order to make amends to his excellent wife for injuries, he must part with her as well as "all the inconvenient pleasures of my life."[4] Presumably, he will never commit again any offence against his wife and there are bright prospects for their domestic felicity.

Allied to the theme of reconciliation of estranged husband and wife is that of the reformation of an erring but good-hearted character. It is often a wayward, if not libertine husband, who is reformed by the patient, uncomplaining forbearance and considerate attention of his virtuous wife. For example, Young Belmont in *The Foundling* has rescued Fidelia, a virtuous maiden of unknown parentage, from an attempted rape. Bringing her home, he gives her out to be the daughter of a dead college friend bequeathed to his guardianship. But he himself has designs upon her virtue. Prevented from executing his plan by Sir Charles Raymond, Belmont repents and reforms and is forgiven by Fidelia.

One of the recurring themes of sentimental comedy is the triumph of pure and ardent love over villainy and wealth. To give only one example, Bevil in *The Conscious Lovers* has brought Indiana from France, and he maintains her in London in the strictest respectability. Not sure of obtaining his father's consent to marry her, he would not even let her know his deep, enduring love for her: "... though I dote on her to death and have no little reason to believe she has the same thoughts for me; yet in all my acquaintance and utmost privacies with her I never once directly told her that I loved."[5] Indiana, aware of his love, appreciates the delicacy of his motives. She looks upon him as one who loves her with sincerity and honour. Their deep love for each other culminates in honourable marriage. Sir John Bevil approves their union, saying that they have set a fair example. He attributes their happiness to their "constancy and merit."

Another favourite theme of sentimental comedy is that of innocent virtue in distress, finally triumphing over male libertinism. The pathetic plight of a maltreated wife or maiden in distress gives the plays a pathetic tone. In fact, there is no sentimental comedy which does not show some leading character in distressful situations. The virtuous Lady Easy in *The Careless Husband* soliloquises in the opening scene that her spirit is broken by an injurious husband. However, her faith in the inherent excellence of virtue is too strong to be shaken by her adversity. She never entertains any thought of deviating from the path of virtue. In *The Conscious Lovers* Indiana, a virtuous maiden, has been found homeless and miserable by Young Bevil while on a continental tour. In Act I, Scene ii, Bevil gives Humphrey a detailed account of her repeated misfortunes till he rescued her from an oppressor in France and brought her to London. But actually her distress is still not over; the warnings of her aunt against the wiles of men keep her in a state of painful uncertainty. Her troubles end when she is discovered to be Mr. Sealand's long-lost daughter, and is married to Bevil.

It is, thus, clear that the themes of sentimental comedy are such as can easily be adapted for the introduction of moral teaching and emotional or sentimental situations, two important features of this sentimental comedy. The sentimental playwrights clearly maintain the importance of a moral purpose and consciously design their plays to recommend virtue and discourage vice. For example, Hugh Kelly concluded *The School for Wives* with the following remarks:

> *Lady Rach.* Instructive ! why the modern critics say that the only business of comedy is to make people laugh.
>
> *Bel.* That is degrading the dignity of letters exceedingly, as well as lessening the utility of the stage. A good comedy is a capital effort of genius, and should therefore be directed to the noblest purposes.
>
> *Miss Wal.* Very true; and unless we learn something while we chuckle, the carpenter who nails a pantomime together will be entitled to more applause than the best comic poet in the kingdom.[6]

The cardinal maxim of sentimental comedy was even more clearly expressed earlier by Winworth at the end of *False Delicacy*: "The stage should be a school of morality; and the noblest of all lessons is the forgiveness of injuries."[7]

Sentimental comedy contains only too obvious moral lesson or lessons, often expressed sententiously near its conclusion. For example, in *The Conscious Lovers* the moral is expressed by Myrtle in the first scene of Act IV by saying that "there is nothing manly but what is conducted by reason and agreeable to the practice of virtue and justice."[8] Steele declares in the preface that the whole play was written for the sake of showing the hero's resistance to the temptation of fighting a duel with his friend, and expresses the hope that "it may have some effect upon the Goths and Vandals that frequent the theatres, or a more polite audience may supply their absence." Sir John Bevil sees a moral in the pairs of lovers being united at the end. Saying that constancy and merit lead to happiness, he adds in the concluding lines of the play: "Whate'er the generous mind itself denies,/The secret care of Providence supplies."[9] In view of the moral and serious tone of this play, Hare rightly remarks that "parts of it might have been written by Mr. Barlow, the preceptor of Sandford and Marton."[10] Indeed, there are many sentimental comedies of the age which have similar preceptual dialogues and moral endings.

Sentimental comedy, as shown above, centres itself around moral problems; it aims at arousing admiration for virtue. This is understandable in a comedy written in reaction against the immoral drama of the Restoration and in response to the new needs of an increasingly bourgeois audience. The Restoration dramatists had forfeited the guidance of a moral standard of which the best of that age had retained a consciousness. The immorality and amorality of the Restoration comedy sprang from an essentially shallow and cynical view of life on which no truly great art could be founded. The sentimental comedy is, as Nicoll points out, an attempt to dramatize a moral problem. But its morality is not adequately realized in the texture of the work as a whole. It stresses morality by a frequent uttering of moral platitudes by the good characters. One cannot help becoming aware of the preacher in the playwright. But a real artist does not seem to thrust upon us a particular view of life. As true comedy appeals to the intellect, there can be no direct morality in it, because morality is mainly a question of the emotions. But the sentimental comedies are consciously instructive. Their plots are designed to work out pre-conceived moral aims. This often mars them as works of art.

Sentimental comedy gives prominence to pathetic scenes. Edmund Burke, commenting upon the pathos in sentimental comedy, wrote in *Reformer* No. 10 (1748): "Our Authors reverse the Business of the Drama and are fond of introducing scenes of Distress in comedy. Who were the first Inventors of this Weeping Comedy, I cannot tell."[11] Although a sentimental comedy always contains some comic scenes, it is the pathetic rather than the humorous element which is dominant in most of the sentimental comedies. Indeed, the legitimacy of pathos in comedy is one of the basic assumptions of the sentimental playwrights. Comedy, according to Steele, need not arouse laughter by exposing a person's vice or folly to ridicule. He even despises laughter and ridicule as weapons of comedy. In the epilogue to *The Conscious Lovers* he expresses his dissatisfaction with the comedy which provokes laughter. In the epilogue to *The Lying Lover* Steele extols pity but despises laughter which he calls the issue of "sudden self-esteem and sudden scorn." For him, to excite laughter is a lower achievement than with pity to chastise delight. The follies and vices are to be attacked not with ridicule, but by causing the public to contemplate with horror their grievous consequences. He indicates his preference for the pathetic in comedy: "Generous pity of a painted woe/Makes us ourselves both more approve and know." He wants comedy to give "a joy too exquisite for laughter."

Steele as well as other sentimental playwrights include in their comedies many scenes or situations designed to arouse emotion, and even draw forth tears. As already stated, humour is not totally absent, but its marked subordination to the sentimental, serious and pathetic is perhaps the most important feature of sentimental comedy. For this reason, Ward and Nettleton define it as that kind of comedy which arouses pity in the mind of the spectator.[12] The general impression is that laughter is a prominent ingredient in the comic effect, even if it does not constitute its sole appeal. The other elements like hope and joy also play a vital role in determining the characteristic appeal of comedy. Its spirit is one of amusement and laughter, of joy in man and the natural order. "Comedy," says Thorndike, "has often been amusing because it was joyous and merry."[13] But surely this is not true of the sentimental comedy. Its conscious moral aim is fundamentally serious, and it appeals to the emotion of pity.

What is remarkable about sentimental comedy is not that it contains the pathetic element, but that this serious element receives much greater prominence than the comic one. It is, however, certain that the sentimental comedy cannot be equated with tragedy, because the main emotional response that it produces is not one of any profound sorrow, tragic suffering, waste and emptiness. It rewards virtue and closes with everyone rejoicing in the benevolent rule of the universe that works out all things for the good of man. But it invariably contains pathetic scenes which are to be applauded on the stage. As Bernbaum points out, the sentimental playwrights "destroyed for ever the tradition that the pathetic must be excluded from comedy."[14]

Professor Coissant remarks that in *The Conscious Lovers* "the action is centred around a pathetic situation."[15] In fact, the central situations are pathetic in most sentimental comedies, and their plots are designed to claim our sympathy for the heroes and heroines. The outstanding examples are *The Careless Husband*, *The Foundling*, *The School for Rakes* and *The Brothers*. In any case, every sentimental comedy contains several tearful scenes. The sentimental possibilities of such situations are fully exploited by the sentimental playwright by according them a prolonged treatment. This is obviously done with a view to evoking the maximum of emotional response from the audience. For example, *The Conscious Lovers* has several emotional, serious and tearful scenes. One scene of emotional intensity follows close upon another. Such scenes often contain most emotional, moralising passages. In Act I, Scene ii, Young Bevil gives Humphrey a very lengthy account of the sufferings of Indiana, which continued until "Providence at the instant interposed and sent me, by miracle, to relieve her."[16] Another pathetic scene shows Indiana distracted with grief when Bevil looks certain to marry another girl. While enumerating her woes to Mr. Sealand, she happens to drop a bracelet by which he recognises her as his long-lost daughter. Having aroused our pity for her, Steele makes it a point to capitalize on the emotion by making the reunion scene unnecessarily lengthy:

Mr. Sealand. Ha! What's this ? My eyes are not deceived. It is, it is the same ! The very bracelet which I bequeathed my wife at our last mournful parting.

Indiana. What said you. sir ! your wife ! Whither does my fancy carry me ? What means his unfelt motion at my heart ? And yet again my fortune but deludes me, for if I err not, sir, your name is Sealand but my lost father's name was - -

Mr. Sealand. Danvers, was it not ?

Indiana. What new amazement ! That is indeed my family.

Mr. Sealand. Know then, when my misfortunes drove me to the Indies, for reasons too tedious now to mention, I changed my name of Danvers into Sealand. . . . O my child, my child !

Indiana. All-gracious heaven ! Is it possible ? Do I embrace my father !

Mr. Sealand. And do I hold thee—These passions are too strong for utterance. Rise, rise, my child, and give my tears their way. O my sister ![17]

Steele has thus exploited the situation for all the emotion he could get out of it. In such scenes the dialogue becomes dull, because the playwright gives full rein to sentimentalism. In the final scene, however, all sighs change to cries of joy.

Thus the themes that compose the plots of the sentimental comedies are easily susceptible of emotional treatment. The playwrights take pains to exploit the emotional possibilities of the situations. Every sentimental comedy contains most emotional passages in its tender and touching scenes. These passages show that often the writing becomes dull when the emotions are intensified in the interests of moral purpose.

A heavy tone of piety marks sentimental comedy. Its didacticism becomes evident from the fifth-act moralizing, often dull. Sometimes one feels that these plays are neither true tragedies nor true comedies. Williams remarks that humour and satire in sentimental comedy "seem like forbidden guests in a house of mourning."[18] Though humour, unlike satire, does creep in, this form of comedy places accent on pity. It solicits our tears for the suffering characters, and admiration for the virtuous. That it was quite popular in its time shows to what extent the play-goers were fond of being crammed with sentiment and capable of being delighted by pathetic pieces.

The fifth acts of these comedies throb with pathos. The pathos of sentimental comedy was defended in its time. Bishop Hurd, for example, wrote that "all *Distresses* were not *improper* in comedy."[19] Cumberland's first biographer addressed himself to all those critics of sentimental comedy who regarded ridicule and laughter as the only legitimate weapons of comedy: ". . . if virtue can be inculcated through the soft influence of tears; if, by awakening the heart to tenderness, we can dispose it to the admission of moral truth, he who would deny to comedy this privilege may be pronounced an enemy to human happiness."[20] In the next passage he defends the pathetic situations of the sentimental comedy by saying that "while tragedy . . . calls forth our tears alone, let it be the province of comedy to mingle them with our smiles, to awaken the serious as well as the cheerful affections of our nature, and to enforce the practice of virtue, by making us laugh at folly, and weep for the consequences of vice."[21]

Many heroes of sentimental comedies are presented as grave and highly moral. The playwrights attempt to embellish them with those qualities which Steele and Addison praised in their periodical essays. Free from all licentious impulses, they are very different from the rake-heroes of the Restoration comedies, who moved above the sphere of emotion, sorrow and suffering. Apparently, they are the embodiments of honesty, constancy, modesty, compassion and benevolence. It may be pointed out here that contemporary criticism appeared to favour such ideal, unmixed characters in literature. For example, the critic for *The Adviesr* No. 5 (11 March 1797) wrote: "That good may ensue from the perusal of a Novel, let the hero be superior to vice; let benevolence be perceptible in all his actions and let him be distinguished by every human virtue."[22] Even Fielding declared, at the beginning of *Joseph Andrews*, that a novelist might do great service to mankind by depicting eminently good characters.

Steele and other sentimental playwrights endeavour, by placing their heroes on a lofty moral plane, to recommend integrity of mind and uprightness of conduct, and instruct their readers in the art of life. Bevil Jr. in *The Conscious Lovers*, Sir John Dorilant in *The School for Lovers*, Lord Winworth in *False Delicacy* and Charles Dudley in *The West Indian* are offered as models of exemplary propriety. Having all the fine qualities which, according to their creators, the typical Restoration hero lacked, they are intended to demonstrate proper morals and manners to the susceptible minds in the audience. Placed in delicate predicaments, these exceptionally moral and refined heroes are made to vent their feelings at great length. They are supposed to have the qualities which, according to Adam Smith, "consist in that degree of sensibility which surprises by its exquisite delicacy and tenderness." They believe in honourable love and sanctity of marriage, and regard moral obligations as of primary importance. They are guided by reason which Steele constantly recommended in his essays as the panacea for all human ills and problems. They have the virtues which, as Steele remarks, distinguish men from brutes (*Tatler* No. 134).

Instead of provoking laughter by showing weaknesses and comic contradictions in human nature, sentimental comedy gives us virtuous characters who embody "True Worth, Integrity, and Honour" demanded by James Wright in 1694. They are, therefore, held up for admiration and emulation. In the eighteenth century Hobbesian ridicule was largely supplanted by benevolent sympathy.[23] Ordinary human nature was not supposed to be a target for derision. The sentimental comedy works not by exciting ridicule for low characters, but by arousing admiration for its virtuous characters, offered as patterns for imitation. We are encouraged to sympathize with them in their misery and to rejoice in their success. By creating paragons of virtue, the sentimental playwrights try to express in their work a better code of human behaviour than that in effect in real life. Their virtuous heroes are finally rewarded as they always triumph over villainy or wickedness.

The eighteenth-century sentimental comedies present their lead characters contending against distresses and finally rewarded for their virtue. This is perhaps best seen in the case of the heroines and other chief female characters in these comedies. The spectators are expected to sympathize with them in their woes and to rejoice in their eventual happiness. A forlorn virtuous maiden is the frequent member of the *dramatis personae* of these plays. She is rewarded for her virtue, but not before her suffering adequately arouses our compassion for her. In her distress she exhibits that excess of emotionalism which, more than anything else, makes the sentimental comedy tearful. Indiana, the heroine of *The Conscious Lovers*, is typical of the sentimental heroines. Bevil's lengthy description of her before Humphrey in the beginning of the play is intended to move the audience to tears. Humphrey exclaims: "Poor soul! O the helpless infant !"[24] Bevil's account of many hardships endured by her on land and sea till he rescued her from the oppressor, is calculated to arouse a feeling of pity for her. Indiana's virtue is no less stressed than her distress. Bevil calls her a woman of honour and virtue.[25] Many generic daughters of Indiana sigh and weep through most distressing situations in the sentimental comedies of the eighteenth century.

The third prominent type of character found in sentimental comedy is an elderly person who is emotional and moralizing. He is the embodiment of benevolence,[26] good nature and tender sentimental feeling. His benevolence springs from the tender emotion of pity which Steele, in the epilogue to *The Living Lover*, hailed as something which Nature gave "for man to man." Often he acts as a *deus ex machina* to clear up the difficulties of the virtuous characters. He looks anxious to relieve the distresses of others and seems to get great satisfaction from acts of charity and benevolence. He is seen as a benevolent guide and friend to the virtuous, apparently seeking nothing for himself. His function is to end marital discords, settle differences between his friends and acquaintances, extend moral support to the deserving, frustrate villainy and smooth the path of distressed virtue.

Sir Friendly Moral in *The Lady's Last Stake* is perhaps the best example of this type of character. His name is an adequate description of his character. He miraculously succeeds in bringing about the reconciliation between Lord and Lady Wronglove. His ward, Miss Notable, speaks about his penchant for moralizing. She tells Lady Wronglove that he gives her a daily lecture against "lightness and gadding abroad"[27] He loses no occasion for talking on questions of duty, right and wrong. As Lord and Lady Wronglove are reconciled to each other, Sir Friendly speaks in a voice touched with emotion: "Age has not yet so drain'd me, but when I see a tenderness in virtue's eye, my heart will soften, and its springs will flow."[28] He is, like Sir Patrick Worthy in Charles Shadwell's *Irish Hospitality*, the embodiment of Shaftesburian benevolism. His faith in the essential goodness of human nature is vindicated as the erring characters repent and reform. "I knew you both had virtue," he tells Lord and Lady Wronglove, "and was too far concern'd indeed to see 'em lost in passion."[29] Mr. Drummond in Mrs. Hannah Cowley's *The Runaway* (1776), Frampton in Mrs. Elizabeth Griffith's *The School for Rakes* (1769) and Paterson in Richard Cumberland's *The Brothers* (1796) are other good examples.

The sentimental benevolent of this comedy, then, often personifies Shaftesburian faith in the natural goodness of man. He seems to be characterized by humanity, good nature and universal benevolence—the ideals preached by the anti-

Hobbesian divines of the Latitudinarian school, and later eulogised by Shaftesbury.[30] His faith in the goodness of humanity and the glory of benevolence is vindicated in the course of the play. He seldom fails to utter edifying moral maxims and precepts in sober earnest, and even with a reformer's zeal. The speeches through which he exhorts the erring characters to just deeds and benevolent feelings are often charged with emotion and seasoned with aphorisms. In fact, his sententious utterances constitute an important feature of sentimental comedy. As "friend of mankind,"[31] he gets the erring characters reformed and the virtuous rewarded, thus playing an important role in resolving the complications of the plot.

We may now well sum up the main points of the eighteenth century sentimental comedy. It avoids the licentiousness of the Restoration comedy which gave offence to the rising middle classes. It is above moral reproach as it has no cuckolded husbands, no adulterous wives, no smutty prologues, and no pornographic thrusts. Free from bawdry or indecency, the dialogue is either preceptual or emotional. Its noble hero or the benevolent elderly man rarely opens his mouth without dropping some moral aphorism. Its distressed heroine accounts for some of the most emotional lines of the play. In the concluding scenes of this comedy, the dialogue is liberally sprinkled with sententious pronouncements.

As this comedy aims mainly at ethical effect rather than mere entertainment, its plots are planned to provide opportunities for scenes of virtuous conduct and to emphasize some moral truths. Its moralizing scenes contain many sermonizing passages with a view to promoting the cause of virtue and wisdom. It treats such themes as facilitate the introduction of moral teaching as well as pathetic situations. It brings out the worth of the traditional values like fidelity, charity and love. In the nineteenth century, Ibsen and Shaw brilliantly exposed the inadequacy of these values and introduced new ones. The plots of sentimental comedy are calculated to show good characters rewarded and bad frustrated. This poetic justice is sometimes achieved through its benevolent elderly gentleman who acts as *deus ex machina*.

The chief characters of sentimental comedy, which is designed to emphasize moral truths, are drawn to exemplify virtue. Uttering pious sentiments, these characters easily fit the plots which are obviously designed to work out pre-conceived moral aims. Its heroes are sought to be presented as models of decency and probity, and its heroines are made to have rather strict standards of fidelity, love and truth in order to serve as moral examples. As the action of sentimental comedy is manipulated to illustrate the Shaftesburian belief in the essential goodness of the human heart, some of its characters are made to exemplify such an optimistic belief, while others are made to express it repeatedly.

The sentimental comedy seeks to arouse emotion which, as Bergson[32] has pointed out, is antithetical to laughter. The sentimental playwrights do not accept the standard critical dogma that the essence of comedy is ridicule. Comedy, they feel, need not arouse laughter by exposing a person's follies and vices to ridicule and derision. By arousing pity for distressed innocence, sentimental comedy is supposed to produce higher pleasure than laughter can give. While it is never entirely devoid of humour, many of its scenes seem to be designed to cause weeping rather than laughter. Often it is with the suffering heroine that the audience is called upon to weep. As this comedy stresses the didactic and sentimental elements, it has very few scenes of joy and exhibition of high spirits. Thus, the sentimental playwright discards the classical view that comedy, through "pleasure" and "laughter", effects a catharsis of the said emotions.[33] The sentimental comedy contains pathetic elements which Otway and Southerne used in their tragedies to arouse in the spectator "generous Pity of a painted Woe." Though its ultimate impression is not really one of tragic suffering, waste and emptiness, yet the emotional response that many of its scenes produce is undoubtedly one of sorrow. Indeed, its spirit is at times so serious as to make it "almost solemn enough for a sermon."

Sentimental comedy was liked in the eighteenth century for revealing harmony underlying life's disharmony, for reinforcing the traditional values, for emphasizing the natural goodness of man and the ultimate joy of our earthly existence. They experienced joy by participating in the situations leading to the eventual success and happiness of the virtuous characters. They liked the heroes of sentimental comedy for their marked sensibility and refinement, and its heroines for being strictly virtuous. They relished its emotional and preceptual dialogue as well as its scenes of repentance and forgiveness. To be sure, this kind of comedy satisfied the contemporary taste for tears and didacticism, and it replaced the licentiousness and cynicism of the Restoration comedy by its humanity and decency.

Today many of us would find it hard to respond to sentimental comedy just as its original audiences did. For many of us the old values have become a "heap of broken images" in these troubled times. Shocked at external conditions and realities, we are likely to feel that the optimism of sentimental comedy is uncritical, that its morality is shallow, that its characters are rather ridiculous in their benevolence and insincere in uttering moral sentiments, and that its scenes of reconciliation are often mawkish. A recent critic is, therefore, right in complaining of "the single-minded artificiality"[34] of the sentimental comedy. The modern readers may not easily admire its characters full of sensibility, the virtue that was so popular in the eighteenth century. Nor can they easily admire a play for "the mere moral Delight received from its Fable," as Cibber's contemporaries did. What Congreve said about Cibber's sentimental comedy *Love's Last Shift* seems to apply to most sentimental comedies of the eighteenth century: ". . . it had only in it a great many things that were *like* wit, that in reality were *not* wit."

The action of sentimental comedies is often interrupted with lengthy homiles upon moral topics and frequent displays of pity. Usually a heavy tone of piety dampens comedies such as *The Lying Lover* (1703), *The Careless Husband* (1704), *The Lady's Last Stake* (1707), *The Conscious Lovers* (1722), *The*

Foundling (1747), *The School for Lovers* (1762), *False Delicacy* (1768), *The School for Rakes* (1769), *The Brothers* (1769), *The West Indian* (1771), *The School for Wives* (1773), and *The Runaway* (1776). The comic element supplied by a few scenes is too thin to relieve their gloomy atmosphere. We find them, to use Hazlitt's well-known phrase, "do-me-good, lack-a-daisical, whining make-believe comedies . . . where the author tries in vain to be merry and wise in the same breath."

It is, therefore, understandable that twentieth-century critics do not fail to mention, in their brief discussions of sentimental comedy, its major artistic blemishes. For example, Daiches remarks that the sententious speeches of its characters "are not artificial enough for a purely formal style and not natural enough for the illusion of realism."[35] "Who can read," asks another critic, "Cumberland's *The West Indian* (1771), or Lillo's *The London Merchant* (1731) and forget that mawkish sweetness, that unctuous virtue, those interminable repentances?"[36] In sentimental comedy, according to Professor Quintana, "there is exaggerated emphasis upon the fundamental nobility of human nature, unworthy acts are too speedily followed by remorse; and remorse leads too promptly to reformation and general happiness for everybody." This comedy, he rightly adds, "preaches insistently and indulges in a characteristic rhetoric of sententiousness and emotionalism."[37]

Though Steele, Cibber, Hugh Kelly and other practitioners of sentimental comedy defended it in the prefaces and prologues to their plays, it did not find adequate warrant in contemporary critical theory.[38] Nor did it stay unchallenged in its time. Several contemporary playwrights regarded it as too tearful and didactic to be genuine comedy. According to them, the primary business of true comedy was to amuse, though it might incidentally teach. But perhaps the most determined opposition that sentimental comedy met with came from Oliver Goldsmith who felt that genuine comedy was characterized by a spirit of amusement and laughter. As shown in the following chapters, he not only ridiculed the prominent features of sentimental comedy but also wrote two unsentimental, non-exemplary and delightful comedies.

NOTES

1. W.F. Gallaway, Jr., "The Sentimentalism of Goldsmith," *PMLA*, 48 (1933), p. 1174.
2. M. Schorer, "Hugh Kelly: His Place in the Sentimental School," *PQ*, 12 (October 1933), p. 396.
3. *British Dramatists from Dryden to Sheridan*, ed. G.H. Nettleton and A.E. Case (Boston, 1939), p. 403.
4. *British Dramatists*, p. 435.
5. *Plays of the Restoration and Eighteenth Century*, ed. D. MacMillan and H.M. Jones (New York, 1931), p. 559.
6. *The School for Wives* in *The Modern Theatre: A Collection of Successful Modern Plays* . . . Selected by Mrs. Inchbald, 10 vols. (London, 1811), IX, p. 247.
7. *Plays of the Restoration and Eighteenth Century*, p. 744.
8. Ibid., p. 574.
9. Ibid., p. 584.
10. M.E. Hare, "Steele and the Sentimental Comedy," *Eighteenth Century Literature: An Oxford Miscellany* (1909), p. 32.
11. Cited by Sherbo, p. 4.
12. Ward, *English Dramatic Literature*, III, 495; Nettleton, *English Drama of Restoration and Eighteenth Century*, p. 264.
13. A.H. Thorndike, *English Comedy* (New York, 1929), p. 11.
14. Bernbaum, p. 94.
15. De Witt C. Croissant, *Studies in the Work of Colley Cibber* (Lawrence, Kan., 1912), p. 62.
16. *Plays of the restoration and Eighteenth Century*, p. 559.
17. Ibid., pp. 582-83.
18. Williams, "*English Sentimental Drama*," p. 409.
19. Cited by Sherbo, p. 8.
20. W. Mumford, *The Life of Richard Cumberland*, 2 vols, (London, 1812), I, p. 281.
21. Ibid., I, p. 283.

22. Cited by R.D. Mayo, *The English Novel in the Magazines, 1740-1815* (London, 1962), p. 153.

23. See S.M. Tave, *The Amiable Humorist: A Study in the Comic Theory and Criticism of the Eighteenth and Early Nineteenth Centuries* (Chicago, 1960).

24. *Plays of the Restoration and Eighteenth Century*, p. 559.

25. Ibid., p. 558.

26. Smith, *The Gay Couple*, pp. 204-11, argues that "benevolence" was an important element in the concept of an ideal person in many plays after 1700.

27. *The Dramatic Works of Colley Cibber*, 5 vols. (London, 1777), II, p. 219.

28. Ibid., p. 280.

29. Ibid., p. 281.

30. See Moore, "Shaftesbury and the Ethical Poets," pp. 264-325, and Crane, "Genealogy of the 'Man of Feeling'," pp. 205-30.

31. See A.R. Humphreys, " 'The Friend of Mankind' (1700-60)—an Aspect of Eighteenth-Century Sensibility," *RES*, 24 (1948), pp. 203-18.

32. H. Bergson, *Laughter*, tr. C. Brereton and F. Rothwell (London, 1935), pp. 4-5.

33. Lane Cooper, *Aristotle on Comedy* (New York, 1922), p. 224. W.P. Ker, *On Modern Literature* (Oxford, 1956), p. 196, endorses the classical view: "The effect of it (Comedy) is indeed a purification of pleasure and laughter and so, to think of it is itself a pleasure."

34. J.W. Donohue, Jr., *Dramatic Character in the English Romantic Age* (Princeton, 1970), p. 122.

35. D. Daiches, *A Critical History of English Literature*, 2 vols. (London, 1961), II, p. 1097.

36. Paul E. Parnell, "The Sentimental Mask", *PMLA*, 78 (1963), p. 529.

37. R. Quintana, "Goldsmith's Achievement as Dramatist", *University of Toronto Quarterly*, 34 (1965), p. 165.

38. See J.W. Draper, "Theory of Comic in Eighteenth Century England," *JEGP*, 37 (1938), pp. 207-23.

4

Goldsmith's View of Sentimental Comedy

Reacting against sentimental drama, Samuel Foote, actor and dramatist, complained in 1768 that this drama was "directed by the genius of insipidity" and that the stage was "a kind of circulating library for the vending of dialogue novels."[1] He himself wrote short dramatic sketches in which he pilloried the methods of the sentimentalists. His puppet-show, *Piety in Pattens* (1773), ridiculed the sentimental desire to idealize common life. In the opening speech the author asserted that "not a single expression shall escape from our mouths that can wound the nicest ear, or produce a blush on the most transparent skin." Foote might have discomfited the sentimentalists, but he could not expand his attacks into full-scale theatrical productions. Perhaps the first great playwright of the age to attack sentimental comedy consistently before composing his comedies of honour and character was Oliver Goldsmith (1730-74). It is important to note his critical observations scattered through his various writings.

Goldsmith seems to have had a very low estimate of the critics, the drama and the theatre-audience of his day. In

Chapter IX of *An Enquiry into the Present State of Polite Learning* (1759) he suggests that it is impossible to satisfy critics with a comedy designed to provoke laughter. He blames them for making poetry dull: "Does the poet paint the absurdities of the vulgar ? then he is *low*. Does he exaggerate the features of folly to render it more thoroughly ridiculous ? he is then very *low*."[2] In Chapter X he maintains that the British theatre shares in the general decline of European culture. The theatrical managers and the critics tend to discourage those who venture to write for the stage. The former, says Goldsmith, are "for decoration and ornament"; the latter, "for regularity and declamation."[3] He deplores the condition of the mid-eighteenth century London theatre by saying that instead of serving the people, the stage is made "subservient to the interests of avarice."[4] For him, the public's lack of sound taste is indicated by the revival of "those pieces of forced humour, far-fetched conceit, and unnatural hyperbole"[5] which have been attributed to Shakespeare. After these uncomplimentary observations on the taste of the critics and the galleries he goes on to remark that "true taste, or even common sense, are out of the question."[6]

In Letter XXI of *The Citizen of the World* (1762), Lien Chi Altangi tells how the spectators were seated and how they behaved one evening at the performance of a five-act tragedy. His Companion in Black, speaking about those who sat in the pit, disclosed to him "that not one in a hundred of them knew even the first principles of criticism; that they assumed the right of being censors because there was none to contradict their pretensions. . . ."[7] Such an audience could only have encouraged bad writing. The great secret of composing a successful tragedy, says Altangi, "is a perfect acquaintance with theatrical ah's and oh's; a certain number of these, interspersed with gods ! tortures ! racks ! and damnation ! shall distort every actor almost into convulsions, and draw tears from every spectator,"[8] and, in conclusion, he ironically remarks that all modern plays must be conceived in the most unnatural manner in order to keep the audience alive.[9]

In Chapter XVIII of *The Vicar of Wakefield,* the strolling player tells Primrose that the spectators have nothing to do with dialect, humour or character; "they only go to be amused, and find themselves happy when they can enjoy a pantomime under the sanction of Jonson's or Shakespeare's name." As the theatrical public lacks proper taste, the "modern" dramatists, in his opinion, need not imitate anything at all; "it is not the composition of the piece, but the number of starts and attitudes that may be introduced into it, that elicits applause." The actor surely speaks for the author when he remarks that "the works of Congreve and Farquhar have too much wit in them for the present taste."[10]

Goldsmith, however, did not compromise his artistic integrity by appeasing the contemporary taste. Professor Ferguson has quoted Goldsmith to show that he wrote *She Stoops to Conquer*, *The Traveller*, *The Life of Nash* and *The Vicar of Wakefield,* while fully aware that these were contrary to the current fashion.[11] Goldsmith's independence of mind is perhaps best shown in breaking away from the current vogue for sentimental comedy. Most of his contemporaries played safe by writing sentimental comedies in view of their popularity. Goldsmith's first play, however, is essentially an anti-sentimental comedy. In the preface, added to the published version of *The Good-Nature'd Man* (1767), he says that he "was strongly prepossessed in favour of the poets of the last age, and strove to imitate them"[12]; and that before the advent of sentimental comedy, the audiences had looked only for "nature and humour in whatever walks of life they were most conspicuous." After declaring his dramatic creed, he hopes that excessive refinement will not put away humour and character from the English stage as it has from the French.

Thus Goldsmith cast ridicule on sentimental comedy in his earlier writings. But it was in his well-known "Essay on the Theatre; or, A Comparison between Laughing and Sentimental Comedy" that he defined in specific critical terms his opposition to sentimental comedy. This essay was published anonymously in the *Westminster Magazine* in January 1773, shortly before the publication of *She Stoops to Conquer*. It was some twenty five years later that Goldsmith's authorship of this essay was established after it was printed in *Essays and Criticism by Dr. Goldsmith* (1798) on the authority of Thomas Wright, the printer of the *Westminster Magazine.* The "Essay" has come to occupy a special place in the Goldsmith canon for being precise in its attack on sentimental comedy which, despite its artificiality, was a very popular form of drama in the eighteenth century as shown above. It is worthwhile to examine Goldsmith's major assertions in the "Essay".

Goldsmith opens by asserting that tragedy which has for some time been the reigning entertainment, has given way to comedy. This is true because the performance records in the recent volumes of *The London Stage* show that tragedy was no longer in vogue during the 1760s which saw a large number of new comedies, both main pieces and afterpieces. Asserting that the sole object of comedy is to entertain by portraying human imperfection or defect, Goldsmith asks whether "exhibition of human distress is likely to afford the mind more entertainment than that of human absurdity."[13]

This observation is not strikingly original because many writers have already tried to identify the comic with some sort of human absurdity or imperfection, rendered ridiculous in comedy. Moreover, Goldsmith seems to forget that there is not a single sentimental comedy which altogether excludes human absurdity or the comic aspect of life. This point may be illustrated by referring to two of Steele's sentimental comedies. *The Lying Lover* which was "damn'd for its piety" contains several comic scenes. But perhaps the best one is the opening scene of Act III in which the two loving cousins, Penelope and Victoria, spoil each other's beauty a little before their meeting with Young Bookwit by applying excessive powder and patches under a pretence of friendly help. This is done after jealousy has arisen between them. After powdering Victoria, Penelope observes in an aside, "Now she looks like a Spright."[14]

Even *The Conscious Lovers*, despite its gloomy atmosphere, contains several diverting things. In an amusing scene (III, i) the coquettish Phillis makes play with Tom, a coxcomb: "... since I'm at leisure, you may tell me when you fell in love with me, how you fell in love with me, and what you have suffered or are ready to suffer for me."[15] Then Tom begs her to shorten his torment: "Oh, Phillis, you don't know how many china cups and glasses my passion for you has made me break. You have broke my fortune as well as my heart."[16]

It is believed that the sentimental playwright Colley Cibber, after perusing the manuscript of *The Conscious Lovers*, had suggested either the addition or extension of the diverting parts of Tom and Phillis. His sentimental comedy, *The Lady's Last Stake*, is not without a vein of humour. The humour in this case is provided by George Brilliant, an amusing coxcomb. Lady Gentle's normal civility to him sends him into raptures. He hastens to tell Lord Wronglove that his faculties are "drown'd in joy."[17] Before sipping the tea offered by Wronglove, he exclaims, "Tea ! thou soft, thou sober sage, and venerable liquid, thou innocent pretence for bringing the wicked of both sexes together in a morning; those female tongue-running, smile-smoothing, heart-opening, wink-tippling cordial. . . ."[18] Laughter is also aroused in this otherwise serious play by the high-spirited Mrs. Conquest and the mirthful Miss Notable.

Thus, the sentimental comedy does not altogether disregard the comic aspect of life. It is, therefore, misleading to suggest, as Goldsmith does in the "Essay", that this comedy relies on pathos from first to last. It seems that the sentimental playwrights did not deem it safe to write exclusively in the sentimental vein; they introduced some comic elements in their work. Nor is Goldsmith absolutely right in suggesting that true comedy "should excite our laughter by ridiculously exhibiting the follies of the lower part of mankind."[19] Mere entertainment need not be the sole end of comedy as there are many good comedies that instruct as well as delight us through the ridicule of follies. In the context of excessively moralizing sentimental comedy, however, Goldsmith's disavowal of moral purpose is not difficult to understand. Hugh Kelly has one of his characters say in the last scene of his sentimental comedy, *False*

Delicacy, that "the stage should be a school of morality." Indeed sentimental comedy aims mainly at ethical effect; it is consciously designed to recommend virtue and ridicule vice. However, its morality is forced on our notice through moral platitudes uttered repeatedly by its good characters. Consequently, it becomes dull unlike Shakespearean comedy. The latter delights us even when it upholds certain moral values because its morality, if any, is adequately realized in its texture. Even some of the modern playwrights such as Ibsen and Galsworthy, although their plays uphold different beliefs and values, achieve at times great success in the artistic realization of their intentions. But this cannot be said about many of the eighteenth century sentimental playwrights in view of their lack of artistic skill.

In the "Essay" Goldsmith quotes Aristotle as saying that comedy is "a picture of the frailties of the lower part of mankind," while tragedy deals with "the misfortunes of the great."[20] He states this classical position to emphasize that true comedy should rouse our laughter by ridiculously exhibiting the vices and follies of mankind. All ancient writers except Terence, he affirms, aim at rendering vice or folly ridiculous, "but never exalt their characters into buskined pomp." In spite of all this, he bemoans, "a new species of dramatic composition has been introduced under the name of sentimental comedy in which the virtues of private life are exhibited rather than the vices exposed; and the distresses rather than the faults of mankind make our interest in the piece."[21]

While Goldsmith has made an important point here, it is rather misleading for him to suggest that the comic is merely that which provokes laughter and that the source of laughter is only ridicule. In fact the spirit of comedy is one of hope and faith in life, of joy and merriment; and laughter, though an outstanding element in our response to comedy, is only an instrument in creating this spirit. Thus Goldsmith's conception of the nature of comedy, as stated in the "Essay," is rather inadequate. This is so because comedy as a dramatic term means any drama that lacks the seriousness of tragedy. It may include episodes which are not designed simply to make us laugh. What is really important is that its spirit should be one of amusement.

Next, Goldsmith remarks that comedy and tragedy are quite separate and distinct genres. These two, he says, have always "run in distinct channels, and never till of late encroached upon the provinces of each other."[22] Here Goldsmith is not quite right because even Shakespearean comedy, though essentially different from sentimental comedy, is not limited to the comic or the ridiculous alone. It deals with life as a whole by including the serious and the satirical along with the comic and the playful. Indeed, a comedy has its own moments of tension though the comic vision requires that the forces of disorder and chaos are finally conquered by those of order and stability.

Goldsmith seems all for the classical comedy which, by excluding the tragic element, remained comic from first to last. He would not have the tragic muse encroach upon the province of comedy. "If we are permitted to make comedy weep," he writes in the "Essay," "we have an equal right to make tragedy laugh, and to set down in blank verse the jests and repartees of all the attendants in a funeral procession."[23] He says that this comedy "aims at touching our passions without the power of being truly pathetic." In this way, he adds, we are likely to lose one great source of entertainment on the stage; for while the comic poet is invading the province of the tragic muse, he leaves her lovely sister quite neglected."[24]

Goldsmith's condemnation of sentimental comedy as an undesirable mixture of the comic and tragic is not without precedents. Sir Philip Sidney, in his *Apologie for Poetrie* (1595), derisively referred to the pre-Shakespearean mixed drama as "mongrel tragi-comedy" which aroused "neither the admiration and commiseration, nor the right sportfulness." He praised the ancients because "they never, or very daintily, match hornpipes and funerals."[25] Then Dryden's Lisideius, in *Essay of Dramatick Poesie* (1668) spoke for a whole generation of neo-classic critics: "There is no theatre in the world has anything so absurd as the English tragi-comedy; 'tis a drama of our own invention, and the fashion of it is enough to proclaim it so; here a course of mirth, there another of sadness and passion, and a third of honour and a duel: in two hours and a half, we run through all the fits of Bedlam."[26]

In the eighteenth century John Dennis argued in a similar vein in his "Remarks on *The Conscious Lovers*," calling laughter and ridicule the distinguishing features of comedy. And Bishop Hurd, in his *Dissertation on the Provinces of the Drama* (1753), had observed that "though mixed dramas may give us pleasure, yet the pleasure, in either kind, will be less in proportion to the mixture." Goldsmith cannot, therefore, be credited with expressing particularly original ideas on the true nature of comedy. Most of what he says here about tragedy and comedy is derivative and obvious.

The "Essay" shows Goldsmith's frantic anxiety to stress his preference for "laughing" comedy over the "weeping," sentimental comedy. He asks: ". . . which deserves the preference, the weeping sentimental comedy so much in fashion at present, or the laughing and even low comedy which seems to have been last exhibited by Vanbrugh and Cibber ?"[27] This tends to suggest that sentimental comedy was the dominant genre in Goldsmith's time and that laughing comedy had almost disappeared. The conclusion of the "Essay" strikes a note of warning that humour is departing from the stage and the audience may soon "sit at a play as gloomy as at the Tabernacle."[28]

Goldsmith's account of the contemporary dramatic trends is not really accurate. The performance records in the recent volumes of *The London Stage* show that humour was not really disappearing from the stage. Indeed, *The London Stage* records many performances of both new laughing comedies and old ones such as Vanbrugh's *The Provok'd Wife* and Farquhar's *The Beaux' Stratagem.* George Winchester Stone Jr., in his introduction to Part 4 of *The London Stage* shows that during the period 1747-76 "Manners" comedy, Shakespeare's comedies and Intrigue comedy also flourished along with the sentimental comedies. A comparison of the runs and revivals of sentimental and non-sentimental plays of the period 1750-80 will reveal that both types were mounted with varying success. Nothing really threatened to banish laughter and amusement from the stage in the eighteenth century. Writers such as Gay, Fielding, Murphy, Colman, Foote and, later on, Goldsmith and Sheridan kept the laughing comedy alive and did not allow the humourless sentimental comedy to eclipse the rival genre.

Goldsmith attacks the characters of sentimental comedy by saying that they are all good and extremely generous, that they lack humour, but have plenty of feeling and sentiment, and that the spectator is taught not only to overlook their defects of character but even to applaud them out of consideration for "the goodness of their hearts, so that folly, instead of being ridiculed, is commended. . . ."[29] This is a good description of the characters of sentimental comedies. Steele's Young Bevil in *The Conscious Lovers*, to give only one example, is presented as extremely virtuous, contending against distresses and finally rewarded. The sentimental playwright encourages the spectator to sympathize with such characters in their misery and to rejoice in their success. Even the rake-heroes of some sentimental comedies are intended to be admired for their essential goodness. Sir Charles Easy, the hero of Cibber's *The Careless Husband*; Young Bootwit, the hero of Steele's *The Lying Lover*; and Young Belmont, the hero of Edward Moore's *The Foundling* are appropriate examples. What Cumberland's Stockwell in *The West Indian* says about Belcour applies to every rake in sentimental comedy: ". . . I have discovered (in him) through the veil of some irregularities, a heart beaming with benevolence."[30] The vices of such characters, Goldsmith rightly complains, are forgiven merely on the basis of their benevolence. They are all finally shamed into reformation to satisfy the demands of morality.

Goldsmith finds it hard to reconcile himself to a typical sentimental comedy which substitutes much of the pathetic for the truly comic. He is right in drawing attention to its pathetic scenes containing insipid dialogue. Every sentimental comedy has scenes designed to arouse emotion and even to draw forth tears. As shown above, the comic, though not totally absent, is markedly subordinated to the pathetic. The central situations in such comedies as Steele's *The Conscious Lovers*, Moore's *The Foundling* and Cumberland's *The Brothers* are pathetic and intended to evoke the maximum of emotional response from the audience. For example, *The Conscious Lovers* contains a lengthy scene in which Mr. Sealand recognizes Indiana as his long-lost daughter. Steele has exploited this situation for all the emotion he could get out of it. Goldsmith, therefore, takes worthy exception to these comedies marked by the stilted elegance of style and the mawkishness of sentiment.

Goldsmith's style in the "Essay" is clearly designed to persuade the reader to his way of thinking. Despite some of its inaccurate statements the "Essay" is important as a direct statement of his artistic intent. It also identifies with admirable clarity the major weaknesses of sentimental comedy—its pathetic scenes, its dull characters, its insipid dialogue, its eschewal of "low" humour and its rigid moral decorum.

We need not be surprised that sentimental comedy was boldly attacked by none other than the sentimental author of *The Deserted Village*. Probably he would not have objected to genuine sentiment and even the kind of ingenious blending of the comic and tragic that we have in Shakespeare and which has been defended by such perceptive critics as Dryden and Johnson. But what he could not stomach was an extreme form of humourless sentimentality which characterized many plays of his age. He despised these comedies for their sighs, sobs and tears, finding them neither true comedies nor true tragedies. Yet the sentimental comedy was so popular that, as he writes in his dedication of *She Stoops to Conquer*, "The undertaking a comedy, not merely sentimental, was very dangerous." He protested against the English imitations of the French *comedie larmoyante* which often excluded "low" characters, and sought to teach men by depicting them not as they are but as they should be. He had in his library the plays of Brueys, La Chausée, Dancourt and Destouches.

Goldsmith particularly despised the French comedy for excluding humour and substituting sentiment. This was perhaps his most reasonable objection to sentimental comedy. Laughter, we know, may not be the sole end of comedy, but it has been an outstanding element in our response to comedy from Aristophanes to Fry. The popular attitude to comedy has been well expressed by Nicoll: "It is the laughter that we look for in comedy, not the sense of moral right or of moral wrong, not the purpose or the significance of the play."[31] Goldsmith's great friend, Dr. Johnson, believed that "the great end of comedy is to make an audience merry." In our own time Lane Cooper has stated the emotional effect of comedy: "The observable effects of comedy, are, on the one hand, a heightened sense of well being accompanied by a thrill of a joy and, on the other hand, a phenomenon of laughter."[32] Goldsmith earnestly pleaded the cause of laughter at a time when, he felt, genuine humour had almost vanished from the French stage. He could not see laughter and amusement departing even from the British theatre.

Goldsmith's contempt for sentimental comedy, his opinion of contemporary theatrical audiences, his remarks on English dramatists and on contemporary English drama, and his own idea of true comedy revealed in his "Essay on the Theatre," are important in as far as they provide a background against which his dramatic achievement is clearly defined. We shall now see how the comic is defined in terms of his own creative art and how his dramatic practice is more or less in harmony with his dramaturgic theory.

NOTES

1. Cited by Muir, *The Comedy of Manners*, p. 156.
2. *The Miscellaneous Works of Oliver Goldsmith*, ed. D. Masson, Globe Edition (London, 1918), p. 439. Hereafter referred to as Masson.
3. Ibid., p. 440
4. Ibid., p. 441.

5. Ibid.
6. Ibid.
7. Ibid., p. 117.
8. Ibid., p. 215.
9. Ibid., p. 216.
10. Ibid., p. 39.
11. Oliver W. Ferguson, "Goldsmith," *SAQ*, 66 (1967), p. 470.
12. Goldsmith's genuine admiration for "the poets of the last age" is shown by his remarks on Congreve, Farquhar and Vanbrugh in "Literature in the Reign of George I" in his *History of England* which appeared on 26 June 1764.
13. Masson, p. 346.
14. *The Plays of Richard Steele*, ed. Shirley Strum Kenny (Oxford, 1971), p. 152.
15. *Plays of the Restoration and Eighteenth Century*. p. 566.
16. Ibid., p. 567.
17. *The Dramatic Works of Colley Cibber*, p. 211.
18. Ibid.
19. Masson, p. 346.
20. Ibid.
21. Ibid.
22. Ibid.
23. Ibid., p. 347.
24. Ibid.
25. *English Critical Texts*, ed. D.J. Enright and E.D. Chickera (London, 1970), p. 42.
26. Ibid., p. 72.
27. Masson, p. 346.
28. Ibid., p. 347.
29. Ibid.
30. *Plays of the Restoration and Eighteenth Century*, p. 786.
31. Nicoll, *Theory of Drama*, p. 193.
32. Lane Cooper, *Aristotle on Comedy* (New York, 1922), p. 180.

5

"The Good-Natur'd Man" as Comedy

Goldsmith wrote his first comedy, *The Good-Natur'd Man*, in 1766 or 1767 and submitted it to Garrick for presentation at Drury Lane. Strangely enough, this shrewd manager felt little enthusiasm about producing the play by the man who was one day to be recognised as one of the foremost dramatists of the eighteenth century. Refusing to revise the script of the play as suggested by Garrick, Goldsmith withdrew the manuscript and turned to Colman[1] who was then in charge of the rival theatre, Covent Garden. Though Colman promptly accepted the play for production he soon started losing confidence in it. However, he was finally persuaded by Goldmith's friends to produce it on January 29, 1768.

Goldsmith was disappointed on the first night when the opening of Act III, where the hero of the play tries to pass off the bailiffs in his house as visiting friends, was hissed by a sentimental audience as "low". What disappointed Goldsmith even more was an extremely enthusiastic response to Hugh Kelly's sentimental comedy *False Delicacy*, produced on

January 23, at the theatre in Drury Lane. Goldsmith, as stated above, had a genuine contempt for sentimental comedy. This is clear from his observations made in the preface to the printed edition of *The Good-Natur'd Man*:

> When I undertook to write a comedy, I confess I was strongly prepossessed in favour of the poets of the last age, and strove to imitate them. The term, *genteel comedy*, was then unknown amongst us, and little more was desired by an audience than nature and humour in whatever walks of life they were most conspicuous. The author of the following scenes never imagined that more would be expected of him, and therefore to delineate character has been his principal aim.

In the context of opposition to his bailiffs' scene, he expressed the hope that "too much refinement will not banish humour and character from ours," as it has already done from the French theatre.

Thus, Goldsmith wrote this play with the avowed aim of presenting nature and humour by delineating character. What follows is a detailed analysis of the play to show that it is refreshingly different from the weeping sentimental comedy of the age. It embodies Goldsmith's idea of the proper function of true comedy because it rouses laughter by its comic situations, pleasing dialogue and amusing characters. We shall quote from it very often to show how it is written in a delightful style. Here the dialogue is an important source of laughter and it creates the mood and atmosphere proper to the laughing comedy.

The Good-Natur'd Man opens with a conversation between Sir William and Jarvis, the faithful family servant. It soon becomes clear that the former's nephew, Honeywood, is open-hearted but foolishly good-natured young man. He went security for a stranger who has absconded. Sir William has taken up the security so that Honeywood now owes him the money. In order to cure his nephew of false benevolence, Sir William will have him arrested for debt and then let him see which of his friends come to his relief. Sir William leaves and what follows is a witty word-play that flashes between Honeywood and Jarvis, revealing that Honeywood gives away to the importunate what he owes to his creditors. The fact that his servants keep on complaining against one another prompts Jarvis to make an amusing generalisation: "Ay, it's the way with them all from the scullion to the privy-counsellor. If they have a bad master, they keep quarrelling with him; if they have a good master, they keep quarrelling with one another."[2] Then enters Butler, drunk, to tell his master that he cannot stay in the family with Jonathan, the footman. The nature of his complaint cannot but provoke laughter, "Sir, he's given to drinking, Sir," says he, "and I shall have my morals corrupted, by keeping such company" (141). Himself a drunkard, he says he hates a drunkard, and then remembers that he came to say that Mr. Croaker is below. Asked why he did not show him up, he makes his exit, saying, "Show him up, sir ? With all my heart, sir. Up or down, all's one to me."

Mr. Croaker is the guardian of Miss Richland whom he wants his son Leontine to marry because of her wealth. Finding neither of the two really enthusiastic about this prospect, he requests Honeywood to use his influence with the lady to persuade her to marry Leontine, little knowing that Mr. Honeywood himself loves her. When Honeywood asks Croaker if this will not mean usurping an authority that rightly belongs to Croaker himself, the doleful man amuses us by his tale of woe: "My wife has so encroach'd upon every one of my privileges, that I'm now no more than a mere lodger in my own house !" (143). Honeywood suggests that a little assertion on his part might restore his authority, but the incorrigible pessimist replies, "No, though I had the spirit of a lion ! I do rouse sometimes. But what then ! Always haggling and haggling. A man is tired of getting the better before his wife is tired of losing the victory."

Mrs. Croaker and Miss Richland show up soon after Mr. Croaker makes his exit. The conversation between Honeywood and the ladies is amusing throughout, especially after Mrs. Croaker remarks in a lighter vein that she knows of none having more friends among the ladies than Honeywood and that one Miss Biddy Bundle is his professed admirer. "The town, madam," Honeywood wittily replies to Miss Richland, "seldom begins to praise a lady's beauty, till she's beginning to lose it!" (146). Mrs. Croaker's comments on the lady in question are delightful. The lady, she says, seems resolved never to lose her beauty because "as her natural face decays, her skill improves in making the artificial one." Nothing amuses her more, she adds, than one who thinks to hide her age by exposing her person everywhere—projecting herself upwards in front of a side-box at the theatre, trailing through a minuet at assembly rooms for balls and in such fashionable resorts as the public gradens decorated with painted romantic scenery.

Honeywood humorously remarks that every age has its admirers, adding, "While you, perhaps, are trading among the warmer climates of youth, there ought to be some to carry on a useful commerce in the frozen latitudes beyond fifty" (147). Miss Richland in turn humorously continues his "nautical" metaphor of the marriage market, saying, "But then the mortifications they must suffer before they can be fitted out for traffic." She has seen, she adds, one such lady fret a whole morning at her hair-dresser when the whole fault lay with her own face. Honeywood is prepared to guarantee that the lady has carried that face at last to a very good market. "This good-natur'd town, madam," he continues, "has husbands, like spectacles, to fit every age, from fifteen to fourscore."

Now a subordinate love affair between Leontine and Olivia complicates the main plot. Their conversation reveals that Leontine was sent by his parents to France to bring home his sister who had been educated there for ten years. But he has brought back instead Olivia whom he loves and who personates the sister to prevent suspicion. By her father's will Miss Richland will forfeit half of her large fortune if she refuses to marry her guardian's son, Leontine. "So, if she rejects you," Mr. Croaker tells his son, "we seize half her fortune: if she accepts you, we seize the whole, and a fine girl into the bargain" (150). There is, thus, a good deal in Act I to amuse us.

The next Act contains one of the most comic situations in the play. Leontine, in seeming compliance with his father's commands, is coming to propose to Miss Richland. Having come to know that Miss Richland's affections are fixed upon Mr. Honeywood, Leontine is convinced that she will refuse to marry him; then he may get his father's consent to choose for himself. But Miss Richland, having already learnt from her maid Garnet the truth about Olivia, has decided to accept Leontine's proposal and thus throw the refusal at last upon him. Leontine, accompanied by his father, at first shows some hesitation in proposing to Miss Richland. We are much amused by the spectacle of an exasperated father pushing and prodding his unwilling son. "Lord ! good sir, moderate your fears; you're so plaguy shy, that one would think you had changed sexes" (152). Finding his son annoyingly diffident, he has to speak to the lady for him several times. Lest she should take Leontine's silence to mean indifference to her, he is careful to assure her that his son loves her most ardently ("there he stands, madam; his very looks declare the force of his passion !"). When Miss Richland mischievously praises modest diffidence and describes a silent address as the genuine eloquence of sincerity, Croaker wittily remarks, "Madam, he has forgot to speak any other language: silence is become his mother tongue" (153).

A non-plussed Leontine, thinking that his modesty tends to attract her, endeavours to look disgusting by being impudent. His disappointment is comic when even his impudence fails him as, instead of prejudicing the lady against himself, he succeeds only in angering his father more. Miss Richland demurely leads them on, saying that Leontine's extraordinary ardour almost compels her to comply. In his utter confusion, Leontine, much to his father's exasperation, can do no better than tell the lady that there is nothing he would avoid so much as compulsion in such a matter, that he would be generous enough to leave her free to refuse. As he asks his father to consider the cruelty of constraining her inclinations, Croaker bursts out: "But I say there's no cruelty. Don't you know, blockhead, that girls have always a roundabout way of saying yes before company ? So get you both gone together into the next room, and hang him that interrupts the tender explanation" (154). Seeing his reluctance, Mr. Croaker calls him stupid whelp, adding, "But I don't wonder, the boy takes entirely after his mother !" (155).

With a beam of delight Mrs. Croaker soon gives her husband a letter from his sister in Lyons. It says that his daughter and some rich English gentleman love each other and that she has already accepted his honourable proposal, though she kept it a secret. Mistaken identity now becomes source of laughter. While the spectator knows the truth about Olivia, Mr. Croaker mistakenly thinks her to be his daughter. He is happy that she is engaged to a rich gentleman but is understandably surprised that the "little baggage" should have kept them all so ignorant of this development. "Yet, I thought," says he, "I saw something she wanted to conceal." When Mrs. Croaker observes that though they have concealed their amour, their wedding would be public, Croaker replies, "I tell thee, woman, the wedding is the most foolish part of the ceremony" (156). Next, Mrs. Croaker tells her husband that but for her he would never have been known to Mr. Lofty who has undertaken Miss Richland's claim at the treasury. Much of her large fortune consists in a claim upon government which Lofty has assured the Croakers the Treasury will allow.

It becomes clear from the manner of Lofty's speech to his servant that he is a vain person pretending to know important people. To our amusement, however, Mrs. Croaker is genuinely impressed by the impostor: "Sir, the happiness and houour are all mine; and yet, I'm only robbing the public while I detain you" (157). Here, as often elsewhere, Goldsmith skilfully uses the device or dramatic irony to obtain a comic effect. A little later Mrs. Croaker, speaking about Lofty, exclaims, "What importance, and yet what modesty !" (158). When the liar tells her that he spoke direct to the secretary about Miss Richland's case and insisted that her business must be done, a thoroughly impressed Mrs. Croaker observes in all seriousness: "This was going to the fountain-head at once, not applying to the understrappers, as Mr. Honeywood would have had us" (159). Then, commenting on Honeywood, he says that "the man was dull, dull as the last new comedy !"[3]

Before long the conversation between Olivia and Leontine, though of a serious nature, is yet amusing because of dramatic irony. Olivia, afraid of being exposed as deceiver sooner or later, is pleased when Leontine tells her that some remarks of his father have induced him to think that he knows the truth about them and that he hopes his father will pardon them. The spectator, however, knows that what Mr. Croaker knows of is not the affair between Leontine and Olivia, but his daughter's plans to marry. So he laughs in a state of superior enlightenment. A little later, the conversation between Croaker and Olivia affords us great amusement. Here the device of dramatic irony has been used most effectively. Mr. Croaker mistaking her for his daughter speaks to her in the context of his sister's letter (of which Leontine and Olivia know nothing), telling him that his daughter is engaged to be married, and suggesting that she be forgiven for keeping it secret from her family.

Olivia feels reassured, thinking that Mr. Croaker has come to know the truth about her but has chosen to be generous and forgiving. Their conversation is amusing because we know that both are deceived, though deceived differently. He complains to his supposed daughter of not being taken into confidence by her in the matter of her proposed marriage. As she refers to her offence, he says he already knows every syllable of the matter but regrets that he is not thought worthy of being consulted: "No, I'm nobody ! I'm to be a mere article of family lumber; a piece of cracked china to be stuck up in a corner !" (162). When a considerably relieved Olivia explains that only the fear of his authority induced her to keep it secret from him, Mr. Croaker, resuming his earlier complaining tone, wittily remarks: "No, no, my consequence is no more; I'm as little minded as a dead Russian in winter, just stuck up with a pipe in his mouth till there comes a thaw. . . ."

When Croaker declares that he forgives her all, Olivia feels overwhelmed by his kindness. He observes that every girl would dissemble for a husband, adding, "My wife and I had never been married, if we had not dissembled a little beforehand !" (163). Leontine who has managed to overhear all this kneels promptly in gratefulness for being forgiven by "the most indulgent of fathers." Mr. Croaker, however, is naturally at a loss to understand this expression of gratitude. "And, good sir," says he, "who sent for you, with that fine tragedy face, and flourising manner ? I don't know what we have to do with your gratitude upon this occasion !"[4] When the excited Leontine insists on enjoying the pleasure of being grateful, Croaker replies: "Lord, sir, we can be happy enough, without your coming in to make up the party. I don't know what's the matter with the boy all this day; he has got into such a rhodomontade manner all the morning !"

It is only after Leontine says, "Is the happiness of marrying my Olivia so small a blessing ?" that he realises that his father still takes Olivia for his daughter. The old man looks surprised and shocked at his son speaking about marrying his own sister. There follows an amusing conversation between father and son:

> *Croaker.* What does the booby mean, or has he any meaning. Eh, what do you mean, you blockhead, you ?
>
> *Leont.* Mean, sir why, sir—only when my sister is to be married, that I have the pleasure of marrying her, sir; that is, of giving her away, sir—I have made a point of it.
>
> *Croaker.* O, is that all ? Give her away. You have made a point of it. . . . (163-64)

Thus Mr. Croaker continues to mistake the lady for his daughter, while Leontine and Olivia are undeceived and will prepare for their elopement to Scotland.

The famous bailiff scene,[5] the funniest of all, occurs in the beginning of Act III. Honeywood is a prisoner in his own house—in the custody of a bailiff and his assistant, clapped on him, the audience knows, by Sir William. We are amused at the bailiff's inability or unwillingness to give a direct answer to simple questions from Honeywood. In order to hide from the world the disgrace of having the bailiffs in his house, he would pretend that they are visiting friends until he has paid off his debt. We are amused by the bailiffs' legal and semi-legal jargon such as "capus" for "capias" (165), and "set in case" for "suppose" (167).

What provokes most laughter, however, is the scene where Honeywood actually pretends to Miss Richland (who knows what has happened) that the strange persons in the house are visiting acquaintances. For this purpose he has promptly put Flanigan, the shabbier of the bailiffs, into a suit of blue and gold and has solicited their co-operation. "You officers," he tells the odd-looking creatures, "are generally favourites among the ladies"; and then, addressing the lady, remarks, "My friends, madam, have been upon very disagreeable duty, I assure you. The fair should, in some measure, recompense the toils of the brave" (168). In the course of conversation the bailiffs fall, much to Honeywood's discomfiture and to our amusement, into the talk peculiar to the navy. "Damn the French," says Flanigan, "the parle-vous, and all that belongs to them !" (169). Honeywood tells Miss Richland that Flanigan being a true English officer, is not satisfied with beating the French; he will scold them too. She clarifies her point to Honeywood, saying, "It was our first adopting the severity of French taste that has brought them in turn to taste us." She has thus only accounted for the French taste for the English plays. But the bailiff greatly embarrasses Honeywood by taking the lady literally: "Taste us ! By the Lord, madam, they devour us ! Give Monseers but a taste, and I'll be damned but they come in for a bellyful ! "

The lady finds this very extraordinary and Honeywood starts fearing that all will be out. We cannot help laughing when we find Honeywood, whenever his "friends" speak indiscreetly, trying desperately to clarify to Miss Richland their remarks so as to avoid suspicion. "I perceive only that you answer one gentleman before he has finished," she tells him, "and the other before he has well begun !" (170). In an aside Honeywood curses the bailiffs' explanations when, luckily for him, Leontine is announced and he finds an excuse to leave along with the bailiffs. The bailiffs, however, make sure that he does not escape by walking one in front and the other behind Honeywood: "Before and behind, you know" (171).

Sir William soon realises that his plan to reclaim his nephew has been upset by Miss Richland who has undertaken to set him free without informing Honeywood of it. He is, however, glad that his nephew has at least one real friend in the world. He discloses his identity to her as also his purpose in remaining a concealed spectator of his nephew's follies. He also tells her that, having learnt that she had some demands upon government, he has been her solicitor there and that Lofty, employed by her guardian for this purpose, is quite contemptible among men in power and is utterly incapable of serving her. This prepares us for the next amusing dialogue between them and Lofty because he does not know that they know everything about him.

When Miss Richland ironically tells Lofty that he has the art of making others' misfortunes his own, the impostor says: "My dear madam, what can a private man like me, do ? One man can't do everything; and then, I do so much in this way every day: Let me see, something considerable might be done for him by subscription; it could not fail if I carried the list. I'll undertake to set down a brace of dukes, two dozen lords, and half the lower house, at my own peril !" (173). He pretends that Sir William is a particular friend of his. About Honeywood, he frankly told his uncle, he says, that "there's no procuring first-rate places for ninth-rate abilities" (174). We are much amused when the liar, not recognising Sir William, tells him to his face that he procured him his place, adding that "no man was fitter (than Sir William) to be toast-master to a club, or had a better head." He calls Sir William's place "a mere trifle," as he "wanted dignity" to occupy a higher one. The following dialogue delights us because of dramatic irony:

> *Sir Will.* Dignity of person, do you mean, sir ? I'm told he's much about my size and figure, sir.
>
> *Lofty.* Ay, tall enough for a marching regiment; but then he wanted a something—a consequence of form—a kind of a—I believe the lady perceives my meaning.
>
> *Miss Rich.* O perfectly ! you courtiers can do anything. I see !

Sir William, pretending to be employed in Miss Richland's affairs, requests Lofty to introduce him to Sir William who, he says, has arrived from Italy. We are much amused by the liar's desperate attempt to wriggle out of tight corner.

In the beginning of Act IV Lofty is surprised to see Honeywood set at liberty. It is amusing to find Lofty hinting at himself as his benefactor. "I suppose, now, Mr. Honeywood," says he, "you think my rent-roll very considerable, and that I have vast sums of money to throw away; I know you do. The world, to be sure, says such things of me" (178). The credulous Honeywood soon feels so overwhelmed by Lofty's generosity that he would even use his influence with Miss Richland to persuade her to love Lofty. Meanwhile Honeywood has offered financial help to Leontine and Olivia for their elopement to Scotland but his cheque has been found not worth a straw. In her despair Olivia makes Garnet write to Leontine for money. The wording of the letter is amusingly ambiguous. It contains such words as "Expedition," "blown up" and "all of a flame" (182). Honeywood's butler who is "drunk and sober ten times a day," is deputed to deliver it, but he drops it before going ten yards from the door. The letter is picked up by Mr. Croaker, who now looks upon himself as the intended victim of "gunpowder-plots, combustibles and conflagration !" (184). He calls the letter badly spelt and crookedly written ("all in the genuine incendiary spelling, and as cramp as the devil").

Croaker's interpretation is that certain inhuman monsters with low pockets will blow his house up and then burn it. In reply to Miss Richland, he says, "Murder's the matter. We shall be all blown up in our beds before morning !" (185). He is critical of the family for not feeling duly alarmed. "My insensible crew could sleep," says he, "though rocked by an earthquake, and fry beef steaks at a volcano !" He later tells Honeywood that while the incendiary letter will freeze him with terror, there is Mrs. Croaker who can read it and laugh.

It is quite amusing to find both husband and wife trying to convince Honeywood how each is right, and each being supported by Honeywood. For example, he agrees with Mrs. Croaker that the best thing would be to laugh off their fears and that it is most absurd "to double our distresses by our apprehensions" (189). But then he also agrees with Mr. Croaker that the best course would be to meet the enemy in the field and that it is utterly absurd "to despise the rattle till we are bit by the snake." "A plague of plagues," Croaker cries out, "we can't be both right. I ought to be sorry, or I ought to be glad. My hat must be on my head, or my hat must be off" (190). Honeywood, gathering that the incendiary letter requires twenty guineas to be left at the bar of the Talbot inn, suggests that he and Croaker seize the writer as soon as he comes there to have the expected booty. The suggestion greatly appeals to Croaker whose reply is amusing: "My dear friend; it's the very thing; the very thing. While I walk by the door, you shall plant yourself in ambush near the bar; burst out upon the miscreant like a masked battery; extort a confession at once, and so hang him up by surprise."

In the opening lines of Act V, there is an amusing conversation between Olivia and Jarvis who has been borrowed from Honeywood to accompany the young lady to Scotland in the absence of Leontine who is obliged to take a different road. The lady is anxious to run away from the inn to Scotland in a post-chaise. But, says Jarvis, "The horses are just finishing their oats; and, as they are not going to be married, they choose to take their own time" (191). Again, commenting upon her resolution to leave for Scotland, he remarks that "resolutions are well kept when they jump with inclination." Next, humour arises from the landlady's belief that Olivia is going to marry Jarvis.

Leontine turns up at the inn in his great anxiety to see Olivia set out safely. While they are speaking, Croaker enters in pursuit of the author of that incendiary stuff. He is surprised to notice from behind his son and "daughter" talking to the landlady about their expedition. The traditional device of eavesdropping is effectively used here for comic effect. Leontine tells Olivia that there is nothing to fear if Honeywood observes his promise of keeping his father employed till they are out of danger. Just as Olivia tells him that his father's temper sometimes "makes him look most shockingly," Mr. Croaker appears dramatically, saying, "How does he look now ? —How does he look now ?" (194). The lovers stand amazed and shocked, but Mr. Croaker, hearing cries without, soon leaves, thinking that Honeywood and others have seized the incendiary.

Soon we behold the extraordinary spectacle of the post-boy dragging in Jarvis, and calling him the incendiary dog. It becomes clear to everyone that it was all an error. Croaker also comes to realize the whole affair between his son and the lady. Later, Sir William, still in disguise, tells Croaker that the young lady belongs to a respectable family and has happily been rescued by Leontine from the authority of her guardian whom he calls a mercenary wretch. Then he confers with Croaker to convince him how he is deceived in Lofty.

This prepares us for an amusing scene in which Lofty is exposed by Sir William. After keeping Miss Richland in suspense for a short while, Lofty tells her with his usual assumption of importance that her claim has been examined and found admissible. Sir William, pretending as Miss Richland's employee, takes the earliest opportunity to inform him that his letter to Sir William was received by him "with the most mortifying contempt" and that he was assured that Sir William knew no such person as Lofty. The impostor laughs and then tells all present that he was in Sir William's house at that time and that he himself sent such an answer to his own letter. When Croaker asks him why he did so, Lofty replies: "In one word, things between Sir William and me must be behind the curtain. A party has many eyes. He sides with Lord Buzzard, I side with Sir Gilbert Goose. So that unriddles the mystery" (201). When Croaker says his suspicions are now over, Lofty is quick to take strong exception to having been suspected. In vain does Croaker try to pacify him.

This gives Sir William the opportunity to prick the balloon of his vanity. He amusingly exposes him before all by telling him who he is: "A gentleman, as well acquainted with politics, as with men in power; as well acquainted with persons of fashion, as with modesty; with Lords of the Treasury, as with truth; and with all, as you are with Sir William Honeywood. I am Sir William Honeywood!" (202). Croaker and Honeywood are astonished to discover Sir William. As for "Mr. Importance," his exposure is complete. A wiser Croaker now decides to pardon Leontine and Olivia. Mrs. Croaker asks her husband to forgive the lovers, adding, "Our own was a stolen match, you know, my dear; and we never had any reason to repent of it" (203). Croaker does not take long to declare that, "if the two poor fools have a mind to marry, I think we can tack them together without crossing the Tweed for it." Sir William has taught a lesson to his nephew who now perceives his errors and would mend his ways. He is also awakened to Miss Richland's true love for him and united to her by Sir William.

The Good-Natur'd Man, thus, not only eschews the excesses of sentimentality, but is full of humour. To be sure, its exposition lacks that brisk vivacity with which Goldsmith's masterpiece, *She Stoops to Conquer*, opens. The latter shows improvement over the first play in dramatic structure.[6] In both plays we laugh most of the time because we recognize incongruities of which the characters themselves are not aware. This ironic atmosphere keeps these characters from being really mawkish. But *The Good-Natur'd Man*, as Professor Quintana shows, successfully employs only irony in elementary fashion; its truly operative ironies are not apparent—they are "never underscored and thrust at us."[7] In *She Stoops to Conquer*, Goldsmith shows greater skill in handling the various ironies that are at work. But although *The Good-Natur'd Man* is thus inferior to *She Stoops to Conquer*, it makes a skilful use of the familiar ingredients of old comedy—concealed identities, misunderstood letters, and scenes at cross-purposes. Goldsmith has handled the complications of plot, the complex twists and turns of circumstance with a remarkable deftness. He not only arouses our curiosity, but also sustains and satisfies it. In lesser hands the characters caught in the tangled web of deception could not have extricated themselves with such naturalness as here. Goldsmith deserves a full measure of credit for his skill in stage-craft that brings these characters triumphantly through to their respective happy endings without straining our sense of probability.

The Good-Natur'd Man has sufficient humour to separate it from *comedie larmoyante*. False sensibility and superficial refinement have been rejected in favour of humorous delineation of manners. Sentimental or genteel comedy had, as a rule, excluded "low" and "mean" characters. But Goldsmith has introduced the drunken butler and the two bailiffs. On the first night, the audience, accustomed to sentimental writings, expressed disgust for the bailiffs and their vulgar language. William Cooke has thus described the episode in *European Magazine* (1793): ". . . in vain did the *bailiff scene* mark with true comic discrimination the manners of that tribe, with the elegant and embarrassed feelings of the benevolent man. The predominant cry of the prejudiced and illiterate part of the pit was, "it was low—it was damn'd *vulgar*, etc." and this *barbarous judgment* had very nearly damned this comedy the very first night . . . ,"[8]

The play is said to have been saved from disaster by the fine performance of Shuter who played Mr. Croaker. On the second night, the offensive scene had to be omitted "in deference to the public taste, grown of late perhaps too delicate," as Goldsmith wrote in his preface. Today we look upon this scene as the high-water mark of the comedy. It is wrong to be critical of the bailiffs' lack of refinement. As they are supposed to "serve in the Fleet," an occasional "damn" is indeed in order. Moreover, if they had scrupulously avoided vulgarity in their conversation with the heroine, Goldsmith would have failed to arouse her suspicions.

Though *The Good-Natur'd Man* is a gay comedy, the traditional Goldsmith criticism views it as sentimental. Gosse, for example, remarks that the play "shows to a considerable extent this sentimental quality,"[9] though he does not illustrate this point. Nicoll complains that "elements of sentimentalism mar its general tone,"[10] but offers no details in explanation. In the same way, Thorndike remarks that the play has a great deal of sentimentality, as its main plot "celebrates the loveliness of virtue."[11] Even a modern critic has pointed out that the play is "seriously spoilt by the prevailing mode" and that "the comic muse takes flight"[12] in the moralistic last scene of the play. Such remarks are unsatisfactory in as much as these tend to equate the play with sentimental comedy by laying misplaced emphasis on certain elements.

What these critics ignore is that a play may have a few sentimental elements and yet remain on the whole a gay comedy. We have to look to its pervasive spirit to decide whether it is gay or sentimental. The Shakespearean comedy itself does not altogether exclude the serious and the emotional. One could trace, for example, several streaks of sentiment in *As You Like It*. It depicts sudden repentance and reformation of the villain, Oliver. And yet it will be ridiculous to term it sentimental, because the spirit informing it is one of joy and merriment. Similarly, the dominant spirit of Goldsmith's play is, as shown above, not of tears or seriousness but of laughter and amusement. Here there is no "repetition and prolongation"[13] of potentially sentimental situations and characters which were drawn out at length in the sentimental comedies of the age. Goldsmith has concentrated on arousing our laughter, and not on wringing sympathetic tears from the sentimental audience.

Sir William Honeywood secretly keeping watch over the conduct of his prodigal nephew and revealing his identity at the proper time of curing him of his extravagance; Miss Richland overlooking young Honeywood's improvidence in view of "his humanity, his universal friendship," (172) showing tenderness in releasing him from the debtor's prison, and then marrying him after he is repentant of his folly; and young Honeywood feeling remorse and vowing reformation, can by no means be called entirely novel characters. But they do differ in several shades from those of sentimental comedies of the period. It is false sentimentalism that Sir William cures his nephew of, and he exposes Lofty in a remarkably delightful manner. Miss Richland, though somewhat colourless as compared with Kate Hardcastle in *She Stoops to Conquer* is not merely another Indiana—utterly pathetic and passive. She has talent for irony as is shown in her conversation with Leontine and Lofty after she knows the truth about them. Indeed she provokes our laughter at their expense. Again, she takes initiative in rescuing the man she loves, forestalling Sir William Honeywood. And it is to her that we largely owe that delicious scene in which the unwilling Leontine proposes to her.

As for Honeywood, his extreme sensibility is ridiculed rather than applauded, as shown below. Goldsmith's characters are novel and comically conceived, contrasting sharply with the stock gloomy characters of the sentimental comedy. Mr. Croaker, for example, is the perennial well-to-do pessimist who delights us by thriving on woe. In Act I Jarvis aptly calls his voice a passing bell, i.e. a mournful bell rung at the moment of a person's death. He is likened to a raven (a bird of ill-omen), a bundle of rue (symbol of woe) and sprig of deadly night shade (142). "His very mirth," Honeywood wittily remarks, "is an antidote to all gaiety, and his appearance has a stronger effect on my spirits than an undertaker's shop." This is confirmed by Croaker's own remarks. It gives him pleasure to speak sorrowfully about "Taxes rising and trade falling. Money flying out of the kingdom and Jesuits swarming into it." Though without any real sorrow, he says, he has cares which "would break a heart of stone" (143). His favourite pastimes are bewailing life's misfortunes, writing about the latest public disaster and seeing a corpse lying in state. Olivia, he is sure, would get much pleasure by seeing old Ruggins, the curry-comb-maker, lying in state, because, he has learnt, "he makes a very handsome corpse, and becomes his coffin prodigiously" (150-51). In Act II, Mrs. Croaker has for him a letter from his sister in Lyons. She tells him excitedly that she has something that will make him smile. But the mournful Croaker seems to know better as he says, "I'll hold you a guinea of that, my dear" (155).

If Croaker amuses as pessimist, so does he as an alarmist. He smells blood and gun-powder in things too ordinary to be taken seriously. We have seen how in Act IV he misinterprets a letter for Leontine to the extent of saying that they all will be blown up in their beds before morning. Miss Richland tells him how he has alarmed the house so often in the past by speaking about all kinds of calamities. "You remember, sir," says she, "it is not above a month ago, that you assured us of a conspiracy among the bakers, to poison us in our bread; and so kept the whole family a week upon potatoes" (185). Though admitted[14] to have been based on Johnson's "Suspirius" (*Rambler* No. 59) the character of Croaker has been so amplified as to impart to it the force of an original conception. Boswell, writing in the *Life of Johnson* for 1768 reveals that Johnson declared that *The Good Natur'd Man* was the best comedy that had appeared since *The Provoked Husband*, "and that there had not been of late any such character exhibited on the stage as that of Croaker."

Mrs. Croaker is her husband's exact opposite: "she all laugh and no joke; he always complaining, and never sorrowful" (142). In Act I she laughs at an old deaf dowager whom she has seen at the auction "bidding like a fury against herself" (145). Laughing at the old lady's great interest in antiques, she describes her as "Herself the most genuine piece of antiquity in the whole collection !" And when Honeywood expresses his inability to share in this good humour, Mrs. Croaker says, "I vow he seems as melancholy as if he had taken a dose of my husband this morning." Then, she amuses us by indulging her sharp tongue at the doubtful charms of a fading beauty. "On my conscience," says her ever-mourning husband, "I believe she could spread a horse-laugh through the pews of a tabernacle" (149). In Act IV, she laughs away her alarmist husband's extravagant apprehensions due to the incendiary letter in his possession. When Croaker, mimicking her laughter, asks her if it is her supreme pleasure to give him no better consolation, she says, "Positively, my dear, what is this incendiary stuff and trumpery to me ? Our house may travel through the air like the house of Loretto, for aught I care, if I'm to be miserable in it" (188). And when her husband says that possibly the tragedy is just beginning, she replies characteristically: "Then let us reserve our distress till the rising of the curtain, or give them the money they want and have done with them."

Goldsmith's amusing satirical portrait of Lofty is one of the delights of the play. This poseur and bluffer is very much like Goldsmith's Beau Tibbs in *The Citizen of the World.* He never tires of boasting of his influence with highly influential people most of whom he has never even so much as met. He has undertaken Miss Richland's claim at the Treasury for which Mrs. Croaker, much to our amusement, claims the whole credit. In Act II, speaking to his servant before Mrs. Croaker, Lofty says, "And if the Venetian Ambassador, or that teasing creature the Marquis, should call, I'm not at home. Dam'me, I'll be pack-horse to none of them !" (157). Poor Mrs. Croaker is considerably impressed by his ability to pull strings with the great to secure favours for his friends, little realizing that his ambassadors, ministers and marquises are the gasconader's own inventions.[15] He pretends to be an eternally sought-after person—"solicited for places here, teased for pensions there, and courted everywhere" (158).

When Mrs. Croaker quotes Waller, he says that men of business like him despise the modern writers and are too busy to read the ancients. Poetry, he adds, "is a pretty thing enough for our wives and daughters; but not for us." It is amusing to find in Act V Sir William leading the boaster on to utterly absurd fabrications and then revealing him in his true colours, despite his ingenuity in making excuses to wriggle out of tight corners. This puts an end to his hour of strutting about the stage in borrowed plumes. And a little later when he makes his final exit, it is not without a touch of self-mockery. "I now begin to find," he admits, "that the man who first invented the art of speaking truth was a much cunninger fellow than I thought him" (204).

These delightful characters contrast sharply with the stock gloomy characters of sentimental comedy. Young Honeywood, however, is undoubtedly a sentimentalist. The maxim of this good-natured hero of the play is that "universal benevolence is the first law of nature" (190). Instead of paying any money owing to a money-lender, he sends ten guineas to a poor gentleman and his children starving in a debtor's prison. He justifies this act of benevolence: "Must I be cruel because he (the money-lender) happens to be importunate; and, to relieve his avarice, leave them to insupportable distress?" (139). Again, he refuses to have a servant hanged for stealing his plate in the pantry, saying, ". . . it's enough that we have lost what he has stolen, let us not add to it the loss of a fellow-creature !" (140).

Goldsmith had already portrayed such a character in his essay, "On Justice and Generosity" where Lysippus is generous to everyone but does not pay his debts. While looking for a suit, Honeywood discovers that most of his suits have been either given away or sold. Hardly has Miss Richland cleared him of his debts when he offers help to Leontine and Olivia for their elopement to Scotland. An embodiment of warm-hearted kindness, he looks upon all with an attitude of sympathetic tolerance. He does not join Mrs. Croaker in ridiculing an old deaf dowager at the auction, or husband-hunting ladies of advanced years. Miss Richland recalls how once at a ball he chose to dance with a most awkward woman in company because none else will. He not only does not get angry with his servant, the tipsy butler, but listens with amusement to his strange complaint that the footman's drunkenness will corrupt his morals.

Goldsmith has thus created in Honeywood a figure worthy of sentimental comedy. It is, however, hard to agree with Bernbaum for whom Honeywood seems to offer nothing but "the commonplace traits of sentimental literature,"[16] or with Nettleton who finds Goldsmith's sentimentalism in Honeywood's sigh in the opening scene, his lapses into gloomy aphorisms and the moral he draws in the end from the error of his ways.[17] These writers clearly fail to see the point that Goldsmith does not like his audience to be pleased with this part of Honeywood.

Honeywood is not intended as an object of sympathy or admiration on our part; he is satirically conceived. Himself said to have been reckless in generosity, Goldsmith had satirized this very shortcoming in Honeywood whose fault is that he loves all the world—every card sharper and conceited dandy finds an easy entrance to his heart. Commenting on his nature Sir William says that it "arises rather from his fears of offending the importunate, than his desire of making the deserving happy" (138). As Jarvis says, he "calls his extravagance, generosity; and his trusting everybody, universal benevolence." By giving credence to every plausible hard luck story, he becomes an easy victim of a pack of false friends and pressing creditors. For Bernbaum this constitutes sentimental praise of Honeywood's qualities; actually Goldsmith is ridiculing his sentimental hero most of the time. A few examples will suffice.

Honeywood's aphoristic utterances look ridiculous in the bailiff scene as the bailiff himself takes them up: "Humanity, sir, is a jewel. It's better than gold. I love humanity" (166). He completely fails to mislead Miss Richland into regarding the bailiffs as his visiting friends. Even her maid knows the truth: "These people he calls officers are officers sure enough: Sheriff's officers; bailiffs, madam !" (171). In Act IV his credulity is simply ridiculous. Though he owes his release from arrest to Miss Richland, he is easily duped by Lofty into believing that he is his rescuer. Honeywood feels grateful for this to the extent of recommending to the heroine the suit of this impostor. Mr. Croaker ridicules Honeywood's foolish benevolence in the concluding lines of Act IV.

Honeywood's anxiety to court popularity by being "too much everyman's man" brings trouble to several of his friends and offends them. Despised by all he is obliged to curse his folly: "How have I sunk by too great an assiduity to please ! How have I overtaxed all my abilities, lest the approbation of a single fool should escape me !" (199). By now he has become despicable even to himself. Convinced of his folly, he cannot but agree with what his uncle says about him: "Your charity, that was but injustice; your benevolence, that was but weakness; and your friendship but credulity" (204). He admits his vanity and meanness, and resolves to save his pity for "real distress" and his friendship for "true merit" (205).

Thus Goldsmith ridicules rather than idealizes Honeywood's sentimentality. Indeed the scrapes into which his sensibility leads him are an attack on sentimental comedy. Sir William is made to remonstrate against his nephew's improvidence. Through Honeywood, as through Dr. Primrose earlier, Goldsmith has emphasized the failure of a benevolent man who is too generous to be prudent and too credulous to see through the guiles of the cunning. His characterization of Honeywood should be interpreted as an attack on sentimental idealism, culpable imprudence and facile optimism which characterized several of the admirable characters of sentimental comedies of the period.

According to Goldsmith, a morbid sensibility renders good-natured persons like Honeywood incapable of distinguishing between the genuine and the spurious. They become, as the Man in Black points out, "mere machines of pity,"[18] and their so-called benevolence is "rather the effect of appetite than reason."[19] Again, in the essay "On Justice and Generosity," speaking about the qualities of charity, generosity, candour and fortitude, Goldsmith says that these "are not, in their own nature, virtues; and, if ever they deserve the title, it is owing only to justice, which impels and directs them."[20] Honeywood's benevolence, since it is not impelled by justice nor disciplined by reason, is a vice rather than a virtue. In Act III Sir William condemns Honeywood's false benevolence. Speaking to Miss Richland he says, "They who pretend most to this universal benevolence, are either deceivers, or dupes" (172). Heilman, recognizing the similarity between "On Justice and Generosity" and Goldsmith's satire on Honeywood, perceptively observes:

> In *The Good-Natur'd Man* Goldsmith dramatizes the generalities of *The Bee*: Young Honeywood is prodigality, disguised as generosity and justified with magniloquence. So close is the parallel that it is difficult to imagine Goldsmith's writing the play without having in mind the earlier essay. It is so tonic and unsentimental that Goldsmith could hardly now turn sentimental or fall short of his intention to use the materials of sentimental plays for the sake of ridiculing them. What he attacked so often, he could hardly yield to even unconsciously.[21]

Several writers have pointed out that Goldsmith was a highly emotional man. For example, Thackeray has described him as "tracked by bailiffs and reproachful creditors, running from a hundred poor dependants, whose appealing looks were perhaps the hardest of all pains for him to bear." Davies has referred to him as excessively benevolent and compassionate like Honeywood.[22] But Goldsmith must have realized how this kind of sentimentality often lands one in difficulties and embarrassments. Professor Friedman shows that Goldsmith had portrayed a man of excessive benevolence on a number of earlier occasions and goes on to remark, "It is not unlikely that Goldsmith's preoccupation with the dangers of good nature came from a recognition of his own excessive benevolence."[23] Indeed, Goldsmith's characterization of Honeywood embodies his disenchantment with, and intellectual condemnation of, such a philosophy.

In his maturity, Goldsmith appears to have come to prefer an enlightened mind to a merely generous heart. Gallaway shows in detail how an anti-sentimental habit of mind exists consistently in Goldsmith's work and concludes that though "Goldsmith was instinctively sensitive, and, in the non-technical sense of the word, sentimental, he was able to keep from being entangled in the doctorinaire sentimental movement of Shaftesbury, Richardson, and Rousseau."[24] Goldsmith's presentation of Honeywood illustrates the truth of this remark. He is a sentimental character but not the one that leaves us moved. Goldsmith's satire is directed against indiscriminate benevolence and perhaps even against the Shaftesburian benevolism. Thus, far from celebrating "the loveliness of virtue" in Honeywood, Goldsmith has ridiculed a typical sentimental hero in this "good-natured" man.

Thus *The Good-Natur'd Man* is in conformity with Goldsmith's theoretical ideals. Gay and unsentimental, it contrasts sharply with the tearful, sentimental comedies of the period. None of them has its comic and satirical characterization, nor its amusing misunderstandings, comic entanglement and ludicrous scenes, nor its lively dialogue which is, in several scenes, in Goldsmith's happiest vein. False sensibility and superficial refinement have been consciously rejected in favour of humorous delineation of manners, as shown by his introduction of such "low" characters as drunken butler and two bailiffs.

Sentimental comedy such as *The Careless Husband* often ends in repentance, the erring hero vows reformation, and a couple of moral reflections precede the final curtain. To be sure, Sir William reads his nephew a lecture in the final scene, Honeywood repents his folly, and he resolves to save his "pity for real distress." But here there is no lachrymose emotion and there is nothing "forced and vapid" about Goldsmith's conclusion, as it states only what has already become evident dramatically. Despite its moralizing finis, *The Good-Natur'd Man* is gay and unsentimental, because it is "wholesome and cheery." Thorndike[25] calls attention to the resemblance of Goldsmith's sub-plot, the Leontine-Olivia action, to the main situation of Steele's *The Conscious Lovers.* But we must remember that while Steele arouses our compassion for the lovers in distress, Goldsmith involves Leontine and Olivia in several comic entanglements. Indeed, it is to Goldsmith's sub-plot that we owe most of the funny scenes.

This shows how a different technique can produce an altogether different effect. Goldsmith's sub-plot not only avoids the excesses of sentimentality, but is full of humour and wit. We laugh most of the time because we recognize incongruities of which the characters themselves are not aware. The ironic atmosphere keeps these characters from being mawkish. As Professor Quintana observes, *The Good-Natur'd Man* "is a true comedy and a fitting prelude to *She Stoops to Conquer.*"[26] It is a remarkably unsentimental comedy as it eschews distressing situations, pathetic characters, emotional dialogues, heavy didacticism and uncritical emphasis on the goodness of human nature. Indeed, *The Good-Natur'd Man* ridicules the sententious moralizing of sentimental comedy and contains what the latter lacks—amusing situations, entertaining characters and witty dialogue.

NOTES

1. See A. Friedman, ed., *The Collected Works of Oliver Goldsmith*, 5 vols. (Oxford, 1966), V, p. 5.
2. *Oliver Goldsmith: Poems and Plays*, Everyman's Edition (1910; rpt. London, 1974), p. 140. All page references to Goldsmith's plays are to this edition. In case of two or more consecutive quotations from the same page of a play, the parenthetical page reference follows only the first quotation.

3. It may be a reference to Hugh Kelly's sentimental comedy, *False Delicacy* (1768), which was first acted at Drury Lane six days before *The Good-Natur'd Man* at Covent Garden.
4. There are in *The Good-Natur'd Man* many such lines of anti-sentimental intent.
5. That this scene, rich with instinctive comedy, was hissed on the first night proved that the eighteenth-century theatre audience was not yet ready for Goldsmith's introduction of "low" comedy.
6. B.E. McCarthy, "The Theme of Liberty in *She Stoops to Conquer*," *Univ. of Windsor Review*, 7 (1971), pp. 1-8, examines in some detail Goldsmith's conscious craftsmanship in this play.
7. Quintana, "Goldsmith's Achievement as Dramatist," p. 166.
8. Cited by Friedman, *Collected Works*, V, p. 5.
9. E. Gosse, *A History of Eighteenth Century Literature* (New York, 1927), p. 317.
10. *Late Eighteenth Century Drama*, pp. 158-59.
11. Thorndike, p. 424.
12. Muir, pp. 157-58.
13. Sherbo, p. 32.
14. See Friedman, *Collected Works*, V, p. 24, n.i.
15. Byron Gassman, *PQ*, 39 (1960), pp. 59-62, argues that in the creation of Lofty, Goldsmith is indebted to *L'Important*, a comedy written by David Augustin de Brueys in 1694.
16. Bernbaum, p. 222.
17. Nettleton, *English Drama*, p. 281.
18. *The Citizen of the World*, Masson, p. 127.
19. Ibid., Masson, p. 126.
20. *The Bee*, No. 3, Masson, p. 373.
21. R.B. Heilman, "The Sentimentalism of Goldsmith's *Good-Natur'd Man*," *Studies for William A. Read* (Baton Rouge, La., 1940), p. 243.

22. Thomas Davies, *Memoirs of the Life of David Garrick*, 2 vols. (London, 1780), II, p, 162.
23. Friedman, *Collected Works*, V, p. 3.
24. W.F. Gallaway, Jr., "The Sentimentalism of Goldsmith," *PMLA*, 48 (1933), p. 1180.
25. Thorndike, p. 425.
26. R. Quintana, *Oliver Goldsmith: A Georgian Study* (London, 1969), p. 147.

6

"She Stoops to Conquer" as Comedy

Goldsmith's masterpiece, *She Stoops to Conquer: or, The Mistakes of a Night* was first produced in 1773 at Covent Garden and was an instant success. This play was dedicated to Dr. Johnson who later said, "I know of no comedy for many years that has so much exhilarated the audience." We may add that it has also continued to delight its audiences ever since the celebrated Doctor made that remark. Written in the tradition of true comedy, *She Stoops to Conquer* stands out glittering from among the many faded comedies of the eighteenth century. Full of humour because of its delightful incidents, character and dialogue, it delivered a staggering blow to the sentimental comedy. What follows is a detailed analysis of the play to show how it is singularly free from pallid sensibility, melting pity and pompous moralizing which characterized many sentimental comedies of the age.

The opening dialogue between Mr. Hardcastle and his wife is both amusing and informative. Mrs. Hardcastle complains that while even insignificant countrified persons go to London to take a month's polishing every winter, they continue to live in their house which is "an old rumbling mansion, that looks for all the world like an inn" (217). This prepares us for the later misunderstandings. The lady also indicates their lack of company in the country which prepares us for the special preparations made later by Mr. Hardcastle to receive his guests. Then, we are amused when Mrs. Hardcastle resents being called old by her husband. She tries to make out that she is only forty ("Add twenty to twenty, and make money of that"), but Mr. Hardcastle gives her age as fifty-seven ("twenty added to twenty, makes just fifty and seven !"). She protests, saying that she was but twenty, when Tony, the child by her first husband, was born. And Tony, she adds, is yet to reach "years of discretion," *i.e.* twenty one.

In fact, it suits Mrs. Hardcastle always to remain forty, as Tony, on being major, will inherit his late father's money, leaving his mother in no control of it. She will always be seen as treating him like a child and concealing his age from him. We are also amused by her doting on Tony. When Hardcastle describes him as a "mere composition of tricks and mischief," she defends him, saying, "Humour, my dear, nothing but humour. Come, Mr. Hardcastle, you must allow the boy a little humour" (218). Soon when he laughs at her hopes of Tony learning Latin, she appeals to his sense of pity by saying that anyone who looks in the boy's face may see that he is consumptive. Their divergent remarks about Tony are quite amusing:

> *Hard.* Ay, if growing too fat be one of the symptoms.
>
> *Mrs. Hard.* He coughs sometimes.
>
> *Hard.* Yes, when his liquor goes the wrong way.
>
> *Mrs. Hard.* I'm actually afraid of his lungs.
>
> *Hard.* And truly, so am I; for he sometimes whoops like a speaking-trumpet. (219)

Tony enters the scene rumbustiously and is in a hurry to reach the alehouse, The Three Pigeons. When Mrs. Hardcastle urges him to disappoint his companions there for one night at least, he replies, "As for disappointing *them*, I should not much mind; but I can't abide to disappoint *myself*!" She tries to detain him, but he soon leaves the stage, hauling her out.

Left alone, Mr. Hardcastle calls them a pair that only spoil each other, and bemoans that in fact the whole age is conspiring to drive away sense and discretion. His daughter Kate enters, making him uneasy at the "superfluous silk" worn by her. She, however, promises to put on her housewife's dress in the evening to please him. This concession to his wishes is an important factor in the plot, as it prepares us for the mistake of Marlow about regarding her as a barmaid. There is a lively conversation between father and daughter after the former describes Marlow as generous, young and brave:

Miss Hard. I'm sure I shall like him.

Hard. And very handsome.

Miss Hard. My dear papa, say no more (*kissing his hand*), he's mine, I'll have him !

Hard. And, to crown all, Kate, he's one of the most bashful and reserved young fellows in all the world.

Miss Hard. Eh ! you have frozen me to death again. That word reserved has undone all the rest of his accomplishments. A reserved lover, it is said, always makes a suspicious husband. (221)

Hardcastle thinks differently but he soon leaves to make arrangements for receiving his guests. His servants, he says, "want as much training as a company of recruits the first day's muster." Kate's friend, Constance Neville, enters and Kate discovers that Marlow is the most intimate friend of Mr. Hastings, Constance's admirer. She is somewhat intrigued by the news that Marlow is "the modestest man alive" in the company of ladies of his own class, though he is all different while among women of "another stamp" (222). Next, we learn of the complications. Mrs. Hardcastle has decided that Tony shall marry his cousin Neville who possesses jewels, but she loves Mr. Hastings, though she pretends to be in love with Tony to keep peace with her aunt.

The second scene of Act I is set in the local ale-house. Tony, seated at the head of the table, is drinking with his companions and singing a self-composed song on the ale-house. It is followed by comments from Tony's "low" companions who significantly show off their learning and refinement:

> *Omnes.* Bravo, bravo !
>
> *First Fellow.* The 'Squire has got spunk in him.
>
> *Second Fellow.* I loves to hear him sing, bekeays he never gives us nothing that's *low*.[1]
>
> *Third Fellow.* O damn anything that's *low*, I cannot bear it !
>
> *Fourth Fellow.* The genteel thing is the genteel thing at any time. If so be that a gentleman bees in a concatenation accordingly. (224-25)

Their merriment is interrupted by Stingo, the landlord, who tells Tony that two gentlemen have come in a post-chaise and are talking something about Mr. Hardcastle. Tony feels that one of them must be the man who is coming to "court" his sister. He asks the landlord to send the gentlemen to him and then dismisses his companions. He thinks of avenging himself on his father for his grumbling at him: "Father-in-law has been calling me whelp, and hound, this half year. Now, if I pleased, I could be so revenged upon the old grumbletonian." (226)

It soon becomes clear that Marlow and Hastings have lost the way to Mr. Hardcastle's and look already exhausted. Finding that they know nothing of the country through which they are travelling, Tony irritates them by stating the obvious after questioning them a good deal. "Why gentleman," says he, "if you know neither the road you are going, nor where you are, nor the road you came, the first thing I have to inform is, that—you have lost your way." Marlow, echoing lines from *Hamlet* (I, v) replies, "We wanted no ghost to tell us that." When Tony wants to know the place they have come from, Marlow says, "That's not necessary towards directing us where we are to go." (227)

Not knowing Tony, Marlow, when induced by the former to give particulars of the Hardcastle family, says that Hardcastle's daughter is said to be beautiful and well-bred; the son, "an awkward booby, reared up and spoiled at his mother's apron-string." This is enough to provoke Tony into beginning the practical joke around which this comedy revolves. ". . . then gentleman," says he, "all I have to tell you is, that you won't reach Mr. Hardcastle's house this night, I believe." He makes the way to that house seem very long, dirty, dark and dangerous. The travellers, he says, will have to cross Quagmire Marsh, Squash Lane, Crack-skull Common and farmer Murrain's barn, before they can discover the house. Marlow remarks in sheer desperation, "Zounds, man ! we could as soon find out the longitude !" (228). The landlord, prompted by Tony, tells them that there is no room in the ale-house. Tony, however, offers to direct them to the Buck's head. He calls it one of the best inns in the whole country, but in reality it is Mr. Hardcastle's house.[2]

Tony adds to his practical joke by telling them that the rich landlord is going to leave off business, wants to be thought a gentleman and will inflict his company on them. We are much amused when Tony says that this landlord would try to stress that his relations held impossibly high positions ("he'll persuade you that his mother was an alderman, and his aunt a justice of the peace !"). Tony's host calls this landlord "A troublesome old blade" but suggests that they will be assured of a good reception. Like him, we chuckle over Tony's mischief as Marlow and Hastings leave for the supposed inn.

The second Act opens with Mr. Hardcastle instructing his awkward servants on their duties at table. "When company comes," he tells them, "you are not to pop out and stare, and then run in again, like frightened rabbits in a warren" (229). We find much amusement in the way he teaches them how to behave. Roger whom he has "advanced from the plough" (230) is told to place himself behind Hardcastle's chair. He is asked not to stand with his hands in his pockets. Diggory is instructed "to make a show at the side-table" and forbidden to be too talkative: ". . . you must hear us talk, and not think of talking; you must see us drink and not think of drinking; you must see us eat and not think of eating." Diggory, however, finds it impossible not to think of eating since, as he admits, whenever he finds yeating going forward, he always wishes for a mouthful himself. He is advised to resist the temptation with the reflection that a bellyful in the kitchen is no worse than a bellyful in the parlour. "Ecod, I thank your worship," says Diggory, "I'll make a shift to stay my stomach with a slice of cold beef in the pantry."

When Hardcastle asks his servants not to burst into laughter should he tell a good story at table, the irrepressible Diggory requests his master not to tell the story of Old Grouse in the gun-room as he cannot help laughing over that. He does not move when asked by Hardcastle how he will behave if one of the country should call for a glass of wine. "Ecod, your worship," says Diggory, "I never have courage till I see the eatables and drinkables brought upo' the table, and then I'm as bauld as a lion" (231). Soon the servants, unused to visitors, look completely bewildered when Hardcastle leaves the stage to receive his guests at the gate. They seem to have learnt nothing from a three-day training, as we find them scattering confusedly, as if frightened, to their posts when Marlow and Hastings are shown in.

This delightful interval of rustic clowning is followed by a discussion between Marlow and Hastings. We are amused by Marlow's inability to talk to ladies of his own class, though he can get on well with females of another class, e.g. the barmaids of inns. He admits that he can never expect to marry unless he were to marry like a medieval king who would win a bride by sending some courier to ask for her hand. The second possibility, he says, lies in following the custom in the East where marriages are arranged by the bridegroom and the bride's father—an arrangement that does not oblige the bridegroom to see the bride at all until the wedding day. "But to go through all the terrors of a formal courtship," he adds, "together with the episode of aunts, grandmothers and cousins, and at last to blurt out the broad staring question of, *madam, will you marry me* ? No, no, that's a strain much above me, I assure you !" (233)

Marlow even says that he has come to the country in order, mainly, to introduce Hastings to the family as his friend and thus help him in courting Neville. This shows that they are unknown to the Hardcastles—a fact that prepares us for Marlow's first subsequent meeting and his amusing conversation with Kate Hardcastle. They are interrupted by Mr. Hardcastle who is naturally[3] taken by them for the innkeeper. This occasions a most amusing ironic conversation between the old man and his guests. His persistent welcome leaves them somewhat untouched. Desired to be under no constraint and to treat the house as Liberty Hall, they treat it as an inn. When Hardcastle begins to tell his story about the Duke of Marlborough, the guests rather speak about the suits they should wear. It is amusing to find the old man resume his favourite story after every interruption until Marlow cuts him short by asking for a glass of punch. Hardcastle says in an amusing aside,[4] "This is the most unaccountable kind of modesty I ever met with !" (235). This is treating his house as Liberty Hall with a vengeance ! However, he remains polite and offers them a "cup"—a hot drink flavoured with herbs and fruits.

As Hardcastle drinks with them, Marlow calls him in an aside a very impudent fellow. Regarding him as a character, however, he decides to humour this eccentric "inn-keeper." The irony continues as the conversation proceeds. He is addressed by Marlow as "old gentleman," and by Hastings as "my philosopher." When he is about to begin his another favourite story of Prince Eugene, Marlow interrupts him again, enquiring about the menu for supper: "What has your philosophy got in the house for supper ?" (236). Completely taken aback by this most impudent behaviour, Hardcastle declares in an aside, "Was ever such a request to a man in his own house !" And again: "Such a brazen dog sure never my eyes beheld" (237). However, he apparently keeps his cool and, when Hastings too asks for his list of the larder, calls for it from the kitchen. The manner of Hastings, says Hardcastle, reminds him of his uncle Colonel Wallop's saying that no man was sure of his supper till he had eaten it, thus adding to the credibility of what Tony has told the visitors about their present landlord. Much to our amusement, Hastings observes in an aside, "All upon the high ropes ! His uncle a colonel ! We shall soon hear of his mother being a justice of peace."

The visitors find the menu much too complicated to select easily from. "The devil, sir," says Marlow, "do you think we have brought down the whole Joiners' Company, or the Corporation of Bedford, to eat up such a supper ? Two or three little things, clean and comfortable, will do." This is one of the most delightful scenes in which Hardcastle's guests dismiss the items of the elaborate menu not only unceremoniously but contemptuously. "Let your brains be knocked out, my good sir; I don't like them" (238), says Hastings; and Marlow eventually asks his host to send them what he pleases, and then insists on going upstairs to see that their beds are aired. Hardcastle feels he has never met such impudent young men, but he controls his temper and accompanies Marlow upstairs.

Miss Neville enters to tell Hastings that the supposed inn is in fact the Hardcastle house. Their conversation serves to remind us that Mrs. Hardcastle wants Tony to marry Miss Neville who has her fortune in jewels. She is hoping to get them soon from her aunt, and the moment they are in her possession, she will be ready to run away with Hastings to France where they can be married. Hastings persuades her not to undeceive Marlow about the house they are in. "I know the strange reserve of his temper is such," he says, "that if abruptly informed of it, he would instantly quit the house before our plan was ripe for execution" (240). When Marlow enters, Hastings tells him that a most fortunate accident has occurred—that Miss Neville and Miss Hardcastle have called at the inn. We laugh over the abnormal shyness displayed by Marlow at the very thought of meeting Kate Hardcastle. In vain does he seek to postpone the meeting. Hastings and Neville try hard to make him take courage to face her.

When Kate enters with a demure face to meet her modest gentleman, Hastings helps Marlow with the conversation and reassures him, "Cicero never spoke better. Once more, and you are confirmed in assurance for ever" (242). But as soon as Hastings departs to have a tête-á-tête with Neville, Marlow relapses into timidity. No amount of encouragement from an understanding Kate helps; his answers become ridiculously incoherent and his anxiety to escape becomes only too apparent. To his great relief, he is beckoned off stage by Neville. Kate, left alone, reflects upon this "sober sentimental" interview during which Marlow scarcely looked at her face.[5] "If I could teach him a little confidence," she soliloquises, "it would be doing somebody that I know of a piece of service" (244). She then leaves the stage, and Tony and Neville enter, followed by Mrs. Hardcastle and Hastings.

There is soon an amusing conversation between Mrs. Hardcastle and Hastings who mocks her pretensions to a knowledge of London and the fashions. She feels highly flattered when he says he believed her to have been brought up all her life at Ranelagh, St. James's, or Tower Wharf,[6] and admires the elegance of her hair-dress. "Such a head in a side-box, at the play-house," says he, "would draw as many gazers as my Lady Mayoress at a City Ball" (245). Charmed by the mocker's agreeable manner she starts criticising her old-fashioned husband saying, "Yet, what signifies *my* dressing when I have such a piece of antiquity by my side as Mr. Hardcastle: all I can say will never argue down a single button from his clothes. . ."(246). The irony continues as she points out to him that Tony and Constance are contracted to, and fond of, each other. She even places them back to back to show they are the same height. In the process Tony bumps Neville's head and is scolded by his mother. There follows an amusing dialogue between mother and son during which Tony complains of her excessive care and coddling of him. When she suggests it was all for his good, Tony protests, saying, "I wish you'd let me and my good alone, then" (247).

Mrs. Hardcastle soon retires with Neville and there follows an amusing discussion between Hastings and Tony about Neville. Tony's remarks about her provoke laughter. He points out that "there's not a more bitter cantankerous toad in all Christendom!" (248). Hastings in an aside says, "Pretty encouragement, this, for a lover." Tony goes on to remark that Neville "has as many tricks as a hare in a thicket, or a colt the first day's breaking," that her play-mate will find her "as loud as a hog in a gate," and that she kicks up at times. She is, he affirms, nothing as compared with his Bet Bouncer, a country beauty with her "two eyes as black as sloes, and cheeks as broad and red as a pulpit cushion" (248-49). Hastings does not feel discouraged but offers to take Neville off Tony's hands, thus leaving him free to pursue his Bet Bouncer. Tony in turn gladly offers to assist Hastings and Neville in their elopement plans by getting them fresh horses and also the jewels from his mother.

The third Act, the centre of the plot, is remarkably delightful. It commences with Hardcastle musing in his house on the unaccountable impudence of Marlow: "To me he appears the most impudent piece of brass that ever spoke with a tongue" (250). When Kate enters, it is amusing to find them talking at cross-purposes about Marlow. But it is natural since each has formed a very different impression of the young man. While Kate speaks about his awkward manner and timidity, her father calls him an exceptionally "bouncing, swaggering puppy" (251); while she recalls his stammering voice with a look fixed on the ground, he recollects his "loud voice, a lordly sir, and a familiarity that made my blood freeze again." Only in one thing do they agree—to reject him; but Kate remarks that if her father should find him less impudent to him and she less timed to her, he could do as a husband. "Certainly," she adds, "we don't meet many such at a horse race in the country" (252). They agree to make further discoveries about Marlow.

As soon as Kate and her father leave the stage, Tony enters with a casket of jewels which he gives to Hastings. He has removed it from his mother's bureau "by the rule of thumb" (253). Hastings, however, fears that Mrs. Hardcastle will discover her loss of jewels as Neville is already asking her for them, not knowing that they are hers already. The plotters' divergent plans threaten to go astray. Mrs. Hardcastle and Neville enter, discussing jewels. The former would not leave possession of jewels until she sees Tony married to Neville. Tony advises his mother to tell her that they are missing, which she does. When she leaves to bring her own garnets for Neville in view of her "loss," Tony tells his cousin that Hastings has the jewels and that she should vanish. Discovering the empty jewel-box, Mrs. Hardcastle returns in a distracted state, crying, "Confusion ! thieves ! robbers ! We are cheated, plundered, broke open, undone !" (255). Tony causes great amusement by pretending to believe that she is merely pretending to be ruined in earnest, that she is only carrying through the original plan. "By the laws," says he, laughing heartily, "I never saw it better acted in my life."

In vain does Mrs. Hardcastle try to be taken seriously by Tony. Like Tony we thoroughly enjoy the irony of the situation. When mother and son leave, Kate enters with the maid. She has discovered by now the trick her brother has played upon Marlow and Hastings. She also learns from the maid that Marlow has mistaken her for a barmaid. His mistake is understandable as Kate was dressed entirely in her country clothes. She decides to keep up the delusion. "But my chief aim is to take my gentleman off his guard," says she, "and like an invisible champion of romance examine the giant's force before I offer to combat" (257). She can do this because, as the maid says, Marlow does not remember her appearance from their first interview, and because Kate can act the barmaid's part effectively. What follows marks the height of Goldsmith's comic ingenuity. Marlow enters musing on his disturbing experience at the supposed inn. We are greatly amused to find a completely different Marlow as soon as he sees the attractive Kate, mistaking her for a barmaid. He begins a very flirtatious conversation with her, showing no trace of his earlier timidity before Miss Hardcastle. Drawing close to her to ascertain her age, he attempts to kiss her. "Pray, sir," says Kate, "keep your distance. One would think you wanted to know one's age as they do horses, by mark of mouth" (259). Pretending to have no inclination to be acquainted with him, she reminds him of how he conducted himself before Miss Hardcastle a short while ago. "I'll warrant me," says she, "before her you looked dashed, and kept bowing to the ground, and talked, for all the world, as if you was before a justice of peace." But Marlow now presents himself as quite capable of dealing with Miss Hardcastle whom he calls "a mere awkward squinting thing." The irony of their different versions of their earlier interview makes this scene highly entertaining.

Marlow is led on by Kate to describe himself as a great favourite among the ladies. His real name, he says, is Solomons, though at the Ladies' Club in town he is known as "their agreeable Rattle." The lively girl thus manages to mock him all through this conversation.[7] Saying that he must see her embroidery, he abruptly seizes her hand. About to snatch a kiss, he is interrupted by Hardcastle. He retires hurriedly, but Kate is reproached by her father for misrepresenting Marlow's behaviour to her: "So, madam ! So I find *this* is your *modest* lover" (260). He is not convinced when Kate says that Marlow's faults will pass off in due course. "He has scarcely been three hours in the house," says he, "and he has already encroached on all my prerogatives" (261). Reluctantly, however, he agrees to give Kate an hour in which to prove that Marlow is really modest.

The fourth Act opens with the news that Marlow's father, Charles Marlow, is expected to arrive at Hardcastle's house the same evening. As Sir Charles knows Hastings, the latter tells Neville they must press on with the elopement. He informs her that he has sent the jewels to Marlow for safe keeping that Tony has promised to provide a pair of fresh horses for their elopement. There is, however, a further complication. As soon as they leave the stage, Marlow enters with a servant and discloses that he has got the jewels deposited with the "landlady" to make them more secure. We laugh over the conspirators' deception now recoiling upon them. Marlow is musing on the charms of the "barmaid" when Hastings enters and realises what has happened to the jewels. There follows a delightful piece of cross-talk as Hastings struggles to conceal his uneasiness at this revelation. He goes off stage, deciding to set off without the jewels. Meanwhile Hardcastle's patience is being exhausted; he cannot tolerate Marlow's servants' drinking freely in his house. When he demands from him an explanation for their insufferable conduct, he is amazed to learn that they have only obeyed their master's orders to drink freely. Marlow cannot understand why the "landlord" should object when he is being helped by increasing his bill. "Were you not told to drink freely," he asks his drunken servant, "and call for what you thought fit, for the good of the house?" (265). Unable to contain himself any longer, Hardcastle asks Marlow to leave his house directly along with his "drunken pack." Much to our amusement, Marlow still at a loss to understand it all, says, "Leave your house !—Sure, you jest, my good friend ! What, when I'm doing what I can to please you !" (266). A little later he speaks to Hardcastle in a serious tone, saying, "This is my house. Mine, while I choose to stay. What right have you to bid me leave this house, sir ? I never met with such impudence, curse me, never in my whole life before !"

Hardcastle soon tells Marlow exactly what he feels about his insolence and banters him a good deal. An angry Marlow calls for the reckoning. Hardcastle, however, leaves, saying he will report this impudence to Marlow's father. Only now does it begin to dawn on Marlow that the house may not be an inn. Soon he is undeceived by Kate, though not entirely. She says she is a poor relation of the Hardcastle family, "appointed to keep the keys, and to see that the guests want nothing in my power to give them" (267). She laughs at Marlow for calling Hardcastle's house an inn. Marlow curses his stupidity: "So then all's out, and I have been damnably imposed on. O, confound my stupid head, I shall be laughed at over the whole town. I shall be stuck up in caricature in all the print-shops" (267-68). He decides to leave the place immediately.

Though reluctant to leave Kate ("you are the only part of the family I leave with reluctance"), Marlow reminds himself of his duty to his father and bids her farewell. Kate, realizing he really loves her, determines to detain him. "I'll still preserve the character in which I stooped to conquer," she soliloquises, "but will undeceive my papa, who, perhaps, may laugh him out of his resolution." Tony now enters with Neville and tells her that his mother has got the jewels again, though she believes it was a mistake of the servants. Neville fears that if her plot is found out she will be locked up or made to stay with her aunt Pedigree. They pretend to fondle each other when Mrs. Hardcastle enters. We enjoy the irony when she expresses her pleasure, saying, "Ah ! have I caught you, my pretty doves ! What, billing, exchanging stolen glances, and broken murmurs ! Ah !" (270). Tony and Neville keep up before her the pretence of being in love with each other. She assures the girl that she will have her jewels soon and declares that Tony and Neville will be married next day. At this point Diggory brings Tony a letter which, Neville alone knows, is from Hastings. Anxious that her aunt should not see it, she engages her in conversation, hoping that Tony will soon make out the letter himself. But Tony makes neither head nor tail of the letter with "such handles, and shanks, and dashes" (271). When his mother offers to help him, Neville manages to take it first. We cannot help laughing when she pretends that it is from one of Tony's friends and is only about cocks and fighting. She urges Tony to put it away as of no consequence. But Tony, anxious to hear it all, hands it to his mother to finish. She becomes beside herself with rage as the note reveals the plan for elopement. She decides to take the girl away to her aunt Pedigree's house and orders Tony to escort them.

Mrs. Hardcastle leaves to prepare for the journey and what follows is a most amusing period of recrimination. Neville calls Tony a stupid fool for failing to understand her nods and signs. But Tony says that the real source of trouble was her own cleverness. Hastings enters angrily and demands from Tony an explanation for what has happened. He is followed by Marlow who blames everyone for making a fool of him. Tony says, "Here's another. We shall have old Bedlam broke loose presently" (273). For a moment he alone becomes a target of abuses from all, and is called an idiot, a poor contemptible booby and an insensible cub. A provoked Tony says to Marlow and Hastings, "Baw ! damme, but I'll fight you both one after the other,—with baskets." Ignoring him, Marlow demands from Hastings an explanation as to why he was kept ignorant of his mistake. But Hastings blames Marlow in turn for delivering the jewels to another person. They are, however, pacified by Neville before she is summoned by Mrs. Hardcastle. Blamed by Marlow for the results of his folly, Tony, until now lost in reverie, suddenly jumps to life, asking them to meet him in two hours at the bottom of the garden. He has an idea for dealing with the situation: ". . . if you don't find Tony Lumpkin a more good-natur'd fellow than you thought for, I'll give you leave to take my best horse, and Bet Bouncer into the bargain !" (275)

Hastings' discussion with a servant in the opening scene of Act V reveals that Mrs. Hardcastle and Neville have gone off in a coach attended by Tony on horse back, that Sir Charles Marlow has arrived in the house and that both he and Hardcastle have been laughing at Marlow's mistake. Hastings leaves to keep his "fruitless" appointment at the bottom of the garden. The amusing confusion is still kept up, as Hardcastle tells Sir Charles that Marlow and Kate do like each other. It will be recalled that earlier in the evening Mr. Hardcastle interrupted Marlow's advances to Kate as the supposed barmaid, and that Marlow already believes her to be a poor relation of the family. Marlow enters to ask pardon for his insolent conduct. Hardcastle, however, needs no such apology; he is quite prepared to match him with his daughter. To our great amusement, Hardcastle can hardly believe his ears when Marlow emphatically denies having been intimate with Kate. "Sure, sir," he tells him, "nothing has past between us but the most profound respect on my side, and the most distant reserve on her's" (277). Hardcastle thinks that Marlow, in trying to be modest, is overacting. He desires him to be open, adding, "your father and I will like you the better for it." But Marlow protests that he and Kate "had but one interview, and that was formal, modest and uninteresting."

Goldsmith has effectively used the device of dramatic irony to obtain a comic effect. The spectator fully enjoys the situation, knowing that Marlow remembers only his first bashful interview with Kate, while Mr. Hardcastle remembers his own interruption of Marlow's flirtatious advances to Kate in her barmaid capacity. Reiterating that he "saw the lady without emotion, and parted without reluctance" (278), Marlow hopes that he will not be prevented from leaving the house where he has suffered numerous embarrassments. The astonishment of the two fathers when Marlow makes his exit, is very amusing. Kate enters and tells them that she and Marlow have had several interviews in which he talked much of love. But she takes care not to mention that on such occasions he never knew she was the Miss Hardcastle he had come down to see for himself. She persuades them to conceal themselves behind a screen in about half an hour, asserting that they will hear him declare his love for her.

The second scene of Act V, set in Hardcastle's garden, is again one of the most amusing. Here Hastings hears from Tony how he has driven his mother and cousin round and round the neighbourhood in the dark only to land them finally in the horsepond at the bottom of their garden. Hastings leaves to relieve Neville, desiring Tony to keep his mother occupied. Mrs. Hardcastle appears exhausted because, as she says, she "never met so many accidents in so short a journey" (281). In the darkness she looks terrified as Tony persuades her they are upon Crackskull Common, some forty miles from home. He causes us great entertainment by playing upon her fears of the robbers. "Don't be afraid, mamma," says he, "don't be afraid. Two of the five that kept here are hanged, and the other three may not find us. Don't be afraid. Is that a man that's galloping behind us? No; it's only a tree. Don't be afraid." Tony, however, soon finds to his own shock that his step-father, out for his evening stroll, is approaching them. Telling her that he is a highwayman, a "damned ill-looking fellow" with long pistols, he persuades her to hide behind a tree, instructing her to stay hidden.

Mr. Hardcastle is surprised to find Tony so soon back from his journey. Tony tells him he has returned after leaving his mother and cousin at his aunt Pedigree's. It is a ludicrous scene with Tony speaking loudly to his father to drown his mother's exclamations of fear from behind. He does his best to prevent discovery, but Mrs. Hardcastle, fearing his son will be murdered by the highwayman, comes running to intercede for his life. Distracted by the events of the evening, she kneels before her husband, begging him to be merciful: "Take compassion on us, good Mr. Highwayman. Take our money, our watches, all we have, but spare our lives. We will never bring you to justice, indeed we won't, good Mr. Highwayman" (283). Realizing that the "robber" is really her husband, she says her fears blinded her but wonders how he could reach "this frightful place, so far from home." She realizes she is in her own garden only when her amazed husband says, "Don't you know the gate, and the mulberry-tree; and don't you remember the horsepond, my dear?" Tony's trick is revealed, and she pursues her unrepentant son off the stage. Meanwhile Hastings has failed to prevail upon Neville to leave with him at once without jewels. He reluctantly consents to her decision to appeal to Hardcastle for justice.

The final scene, set in Hardcastle's house, clears up all complications in a highly entertaining manner. It opens with conversation between Kate and Sir Charles. She has directed him how to conceal himself along with her father in order to overhear Marlow declare his love for her. As he leaves to fetch Hardcastle, Marlow enters to take leave of Kate whom he still believes to be the poor relation of the family. Though in love with her, he sees little possibility of marrying one so inferior to him in rank. Kate accuses him having no real love for her, saying, "I must have only the mockery of your addresses, while all your serious aims are fixed on fortune" (285). At this point Sir Charles and Hardcastle are seen concealing themselves behind the screen. They soon overhear Marlow admiring Kate's beauty and declaring his love for her. "By all that's good," says he, "I can have no happiness but what's in your power to grant me" (286). He will even stay in the house to atone for the levity of his conduct. When he goes on his knees to press his point, the old men, amazed at his conduct, appear to reproach him for having deceived them. Marlow now realises the real identity of "poor relation." Highly embarrassed by his impudence and teased by the lively Kate, he thinks of making his escape but is prevailed upon by Hardcastle to stay, and all is forgiven.

Mrs. Hardcastle enters with Tony to say that by eloping with Hastings Neville has forfeited her right to her fortune. She can have her jewels only if Tony, when of age, refuses to marry her. But Mr. Hardcastle resolves this complication soon after Hastings and Neville return unexpectedly. He declares that Tony is already of age. The first use Tony makes of his liberty is to refuse to marry Neville so that he can marry his Bet Bouncer. As Kate will marry Marlow, She has successfully "Stooped to conquer." The mistakes of the night thus end in rejoicing for everybody. The "laughing" comedy ends with Hardcastle's saying to Marlow: ". . . so boy, take her (Kate); as you have been mistaken in the mistress, my wish is, that you may never be mistaken in the wife."

Thus, *She Stoops to Conquer* is throughout a hilarious comedy eschewing tears and reforms. Laughter, as Thorndike says, "shifts from one person to another like the box of Miss Neville's jewels, which is ever being won and lost."[8] The chief diversion arises, of course, from Tony's clever stratagem on Marlow. But how many can really make this humorous incident the mainspring of such a laughing comedy ? Sick of the weeping comedies of the period, Goldsmith's primary aim was to amuse; he has done it by means of a most skilful manipulation of plot, a gay and racy dialogue and, as shown below, highly entertaining characters. The amusing situations are incorporated into an inevitable plot. The dialogue, as we have seen, is singularly free of the maudlin verbiage of the sentimentalists.

Someone in quest of sentimentality may claim to notice it towards the conclusion of the play where Hastings and Neville decide against elopement and appeal to Mr. Hardcastle for mercy. "But I'm now recovered from the delusion," says Neville, "and hope from your tenderness what is denied me from a nearer connection" (288). This causes Mrs. Hardcastle to remark, "Pshaw; pshaw ! this is all but the whining end of a modern novel." As shown above, Hardcastle promptly brings about a happy resolution by declaring Tony to be of age. It will be absurd to single out such an incident as evidence of Goldsmith's sentimentalism from a play in which the spirit of merriment is never extinguished. The psychology of comedy requires that all should be set rightly, and Goldsmith cannot be accused of sentimentalism for using one of the traditional devices to produce the maximum of joy.

The detective of sentimentalism may also find a sentimental bias where Marlow's intentions towards Kate are revealed as honourable when he still believes her to be Hardcastle's poor realtion: "By heavens, madam," he tells her, "fortune was ever my smallest consideration. Your beauty at first caught my eye; for who could see that without emotion ? . . . What at first seemed rustic plainness, now appears refined simplicity. What seemed forward assurance, now strikes me as the result of courageous innocence, and conscious virtue" (285). But actually it is comic rather than sentimental because of our constant awareness that Hardcastle and Sir Charles are eavesdropping upon the scene. Soon Kate laughs at Marlow by declaring that she is Hardcastle's daughter to whom he spoke a short while ago as "the mild, modest, sentimental man of gravity" (287). Earlier,in Act IV, Marlow expressed his affection for Kate with "By heaven, she weeps" (286). But we should not forget that Kate was peeping through her fingers at him and was only pretending to cry.

What remains to be stressed is Goldsmith's characterization which, perhaps more than any other thing, separates the play from the sentimental comedy. There are no serious, gloomy, weeping or moralizing characters; all are comically conceived and it is through speech that they reveal so much of themselves.

We laugh *with* Tony and Kate, especially with the former; we laugh *at* Mrs. Hardcastle and Marlow, especially at the latter. Amusing, too, are Mr. Hardcastle, Hastings and Neville. But it is important to stress that Goldsmith, as Forster has pointed out, "does not snatch a joke out of a misery, or an ugliness, or a mortification, or anything that, apart from the joke, would be likely to give pain. . . ."[9] It will be remembered that Aristote had said, "It (the ludicrous) consists in some defect or ugliness which is not painful or destructive."

Mr. Hardcastle, the plain country gentleman, is not likely to give up his old-fashioned ideas. Living in his old-fashioned house, he says in the opening scene, "I love everything that's old: old friends, old times, old manners, old books, old wine. . . " (218). We laugh over his talkativeness, his elaborate instructions to servants and his fondness for long-winded stories. What amuses us most, however, is his utter astonishment at the strange behaviour of Marlow whose error he does not perceive. Commenting on his impudence he remarks in an aside, "This may be modern modesty, but I never saw anything look so like old-fashioned impudence" (239). Later, of course, he laughs heartily over Marlow's mistake.

Mrs. Hardcastle, so different from her husband, is presented as a ridiculous lady. She complains of a life spent in the country and would, if she could, "take a trip to town now and then, to rub off the rust little" (218). She complains to her husband that their entertainment is confined to his old stories of Prince Eugene and the Duke of Marlborough. We have seen her being completely taken in by the flattery of Hastings who knows her eagerness to follow the London fashions. Indulgent to her son, she wrongly thinks he is consumptive, and would give him no education for fear of damaging his health. Education, she thinks, is even unnecessary in his case. "I don't think," she says in the opening scene, "a boy wants much learning to spend fifteen hundred a year" (218). We laugh at her gullibility. Tony and Neville, especially the former, often deceive her easily. Again, though she stands on her own ground, she is duped by Tony into believing that she is upon Crackskull

Common, the most notorious spot in the country. She provokes our laughter by kneeling before her husband, taking him for a highwayman.

Hastings and Neville, while they are dramatically less interesting than Marlow and Kate, are much more interesting than the gloomy, moralizing lovers of the sentimental comedy. They decide not to disabuse Marlow of the real identity of the supposed innkeeper. Hastings, says Marlow, has "talents and art to captivate any woman" (233). He is amused by Marlow's awkwardness during his first interview with Kate, but helps him with the conversation for some time, making delightful comments in the process. He also amuses us by his clever mockery of Mrs. Hardcastle's pretensions to a knowledge of London, as the flattered lady does not realize he is simply making a fool of her. As for Miss Neville, though prudence dictates her conduct, she is much different from the pathetic heroines of the sentimental comedy. She practises dissimulation to avoid oppression. She befools her aunt by making a show of affection for Tony. She amuses us by taking Hastings' letter from Tony, pretending before her aunt it comes from one of Tony's friends, and inventing material as she reads it. Tony tells his mother that he "always loved cousin Con's hazel eyes, and her pretty long fingers. . ." (270).

The delightful Kate offers a refreshing contrast with the bloodless heroines of the sentimental comedy. We have already seen how her enthusiasm for Marlow is dampened on learning that he is also bashful and reserved, and how she laughs heartily over Marlow's "sober, sentimental interview" with her. She has, like Shakespeare's Rosalind, a keen sense of fun coupled with a clever brain. She shows a ready wit and a lively sense of humour in her role as barmaid and thoroughly enjoys the comedy of curing Marlow of his timidity. In Act III when she finds that Marlow has mistaken her for barmaid, she resolves to keep up the delusion: "Tell me, Pimple," she asks the maid, "how do you like my present dress ? Don't you think I look something like Cherry in the *Beaux' Stratagem* ?" When Marlow, finding her vastly handsome and taking fancy to her sprightly malicious eye, asks for the nectar of her lips, she looks remarkably natural in her pretence that he is asking for some kind of liquor: "Nectar ! nectar ! that's a liquor there's no call for in these parts. French, I suppose. We keep no French wines here, sir" (258). As shown above, she makes him look ridiculous throughout this scene. In Act IV, seeing that Marlow has begun to realize his misake, she tells him that he is at Mr. Hardcastle's house and not at an inn. But as it is still early to undeceive him about her identity, the gay girl displays a ready inventiveness by telling him she is a poor relation of the family. She knows how to deal with the situation she has brought about out of sense of fun. We see this (Act V, Scene iii) in the way she enables her father and Sir Charles to overhear Marlow's declaration of love for her. In the same scene she shows a sheer genius for teasing Marlow when he discovers her identity. She banters him about his dual character, tormenting him to the back scene.

We are much amused by Marlow as he is a very singular character indeed. Bashful before ladies of his own class, he is extremely forward with those of lower class; he is quite aware of his curious lack of assurance when dealing with the former. In Act II, he admits to Hastings that women of reputation "freeze" and "petrify" him; a modest woman in her gay and elegant dress is to him "the most tremendous object of the whole creation" (232). Nor does he ever quite hope to marry unless it is to be a marriage by proxy. "This stammer in my address," he tells Hastings, "and this awkward prepossessing visage of mine, can never permit me to soar above the reach of a milliner's apprentice, or one of the duchesses of Drury Lane" (233). We laugh at his awkward *mauvaise honte* in his first interview with Kate during which he desperately relies on Hastings to save himself from looking confoundedly ridiculous. Left alone with Kate, he is overcome with a strange nervousness and his powers of conversation desert him. This bashfulness contrasts sharply with his subsequent boldness in relation to the same girl when he mistakes her for a barmaid. We see him hauling his "pretty maid " before he is interrupted by an amazed Hardcastle. Like Mrs. Hardcastle, he is the gull of the comedy. The dupe of

Tony, he continues to treat Hardcastle as innkeeper until his host threatens to report his impudence to his father. He is equally easily duped by Kate whom he first believes to be a barmaid, and later, a poor relation of the Hardcastle family. Finally, when he is completely undeceived, it is a manner most embarrassing to him. Bantered by Kate, he curses his noisy head, adding, "I never attempted to be impudent yet, that I was not taken down"(287).

It is in Tony, however, that the heart of comedy beats. We owe him most of the fun and mirth of the play which revolves around his practical joke on Marlow and Hastings. The central positioning of such a character in the action of any play will act as a sufficient check upon mawkishness. Full of mischievous humour, he is accurately described by Mr. Hardcastle as "A mere composition of tricks and mischief!" (218). The old man himself is one of his victims. "It was but yesterday he fastened my wig to the back of my chair,"[10] he tells Mrs. Hardcastle, "and when I went to make a bow, I popped my bald head in Mrs. Frizzle's face !" (218). He has been spoilt by the excessive mothering of Mrs. Hardcastle who has been, as Neville says, "setting off her pretty monster as the very pink of perfection" (223). He spends most of his time with his pot companions in the alehouse. Money is no problem for him. "If I had not a key to every drawer in mother's bureau," he tells Hastings, "how could I go to the alehouse so often as I do ?" (253). As he resents his step-father's grumbling at his drinking habits, he directs Marlow and Hastings to his house as to an inn. His mother is another prominent victim of his practical joking. He conspires against her by working for the elopement of the lovers, Neville and Hastings. He removes from her bureau the casket containing Neville's jewels, encourages her to pretend that they are missing and, when she discovers that they have really vanished, he pretends that she is pretending they are missing.

When Mrs. Hardcastle discovers the whole conspiracy and orders Tony to escort her and Neville to Neville's aunt Pedigree, he hits on a most amusing stratagem. He drives his mother and cousin round and round the neighbourhood in the dark and finally lands them in the horsepond at the bottom of their garden. We have seen how he alarms his mother into a hysterical state with a variety of roguish tricks. We don't sympathise with her because she has been presented as a foolish and vain woman prompted by ignoble motives. Tony's deception revealed, he justifies his conduct before his mother, saying, "Ecod, mother, all the parish says you have spoiled me, and so you may take the fruits on't" (283). Mr. Hardcastle signficantly remarks that there is morality in Tony's reply. Tony does not mind offending her: "I don't value her resentment the bounce of a cracker." At the end, thanks to Mr. Hardcastle, he frees himself from her apron-strings and can pursue his Betty Bouncer. It is very largely Tony and Kate who keep the comedy in the Shakespearean tradition.

The total impression of *She Stoops to Conquer* as a result of its situations, characters and language is, thus, one of laughing comedy as opposed to that of weeping comedy which Goldsmith attacked in his "Essay on the Theatre." The opinion of contemporaneity can sometime be so faulty as to seem grotesque to later generations. The aristocratic Horace Walpole, in a letter to his friend Mason, delivered himself of a judgment which most of us will find hard to understand. Calling the play " the lowest of all farces," he condemned the "execution" of Goldsmith's plan: "The drift tends to no moral, no edification of any kind; the situations, however, are well imagined, and make one laugh in spite of the grossness of the dialogue, the forced witticisms, and total improbability of the whole plan and conduct. But what disgusts me most is that, though the characters are very low, and aim at low humour, not one of them says a sentence that is natural or marks any character at all."[11] Perhaps nothing more is needed to prove Walpole's partiality to sentimental comedy of which Goldsmith's play is the direct opposite. Goldsmith had anticipated such criticism as Walpole's. In an epilogue at one time intended for the play, he wrote:

> Without a star, a coronet or garter,
> How can the piece expect or hope for quarter ?
> No high-life scenes, no sentiment:—the creature
> Still stoops among the low to copy nature.

The last line defends Goldsmith's approach; his drama, as of course Shakespeare's, holds the mirror up to nature.

She Stoops to Conquer cannot be labelled low farce, even if several of its incidents look farcical and Tony is a "low" comic creation. Goldsmith's dramatic construction of incident is admirable. As Dr. Johnson said, "the incidents are so prepared as not to seem improbable." The characters are by no means superficial; well thought out, they show natural consistency. We can recognize, and identify ourselves with, Mr. and Mrs. Hardcastle, Tony and Marlow. While the play makes us roar with laughter, it is free from any slapstick buffoonery. Goldsmith's comic muse is not easily definable. She is neither satirical like Jonson's, nor sentimental like Cumberland's, nor even romantic like Shakespeare's. As Thorndike points out, "She has a special fondness for practical jokes but she is not merely a romp."[12] Unlike the sentimental playwrights, Goldsmith has no didactic intention. This lack of edification of which Walpole complains, and a humorous view of life separate Goldsmith's comedy from those mawkish comedies of the age, which are heavy with dull moralizing. Again, Walpole's complaint of "low" characters is ill-founded. As Goldsmith aims at drawing nature and character, he boldly puts the low upon the stage. In *The Good-Natur'd Man*, the bailiff scene best expresses Goldsmith's disapproval of the sentimental mode, though it was hissed as low by its audience at Covent Garden.

Tony, too, would be low to an audience used to sentimental comedies. But it is he who is the most delightful character in the play. Like Shakespeare's Puck he laughs heartily at the follies of his victims. It is significant that he is not held as an example of bad behaviour or finished as a reformed character. Nor would we like the play to be without honest Diggory who asks for his accustomed licence to laugh at Hardcastle's story of Ould Grouse in the gun-room. Also, Goldsmith's is not Walpole's "nature." For Goldsmith, "the natural" means "the avoidance of anything like falsification and affected sophistication in art." Another critic, William Woodfall, was also unfair to Goldsmith's play. He wrote in irritation in the *Monthly Review* (March 1773): "The fable of *She Stoops to Conquer* is a series of blunders, which the Author calls the *Mistakes of a Night*; but they are such mistakes as never were made, and we believe, never could have been committed."[13] He went on to list several incidents of the play as most improbable, forgetting that Goldsmith adequately hints in the beginning at whatever happens later.

It hardly needs to be stressed that the conventions of comedy seldom coincide with those of real life. Woodfall found almost all the incidents at the supposed inn most improbable. Many of us, however, find them no more improbable than those numerous blunders and involvements which comedy has often exhibited. Those who accuse Goldsmith's plot of straining the bounds of probability would do well to remember that its most preposterous incident, the mistaking of a country gentleman's house for an inn, was suggested, according to Goldsmith's sister, Mrs. Hodson, by an actual experience of Goldsmith. In any case, the so-called improbabilities of *She Stoops to Conquer* do not detract from its effectiveness as a stage play.

Thus, *She Stoops to Conquer* is suffused with a spirit of merriment which is the chief foe of didactic sentimentality. Although *The Good-Natur'd Man*, too, eschews the emotional excesses of sentimental comedy, it is *She Stoops to Conquer* which shows Goldsmith's comic skills at their best. The latter shows great improvement over the former in embodying his theory of comedy, stated in his "Essay on the Theatre." As shown in Chapter 4 above, the "Essay" is the *locus classicus* for Goldsmith's objection to *comédie larmoyante*.

Characterized by its delightful scenes, characters and dialogue, *She Stoops to Conquer* brilliantly sustains the dramatic interest throughout by means of a series of effective stage situations. The play is, therefore, in sharp contrast to the sentimental comedy which Goldsmith regarded as a bastard version of tragedy in view of its pathetic scenes, serious charac-rest and dull speeches.

Ironically, Colman, the manager of Covent Garden Theatre, feared that *She Stoops to Conquer* would not please its audience. He did not stage it until he was persuaded to do so by Dr. Johnson "by much solicitation, nay, a kind of force."[14] As the curtain rose, Woodward repeated in simperingly pathetic tones Garrick's mock monody on the imminent death of comedy:

Pray would you know the reason why I'm crying ?
The Comic Muse, long sick, is now a-dying !
To *her* a mawkish drab of spurious breed,
Who deals in sentimentals will succeed !

Cumberland, the leader of the sentimental school, tells us in his *Memoirs* how the formidable Dr. Johnson sat in front of a side-box, because, such was his reputation, "when he laughed, everybody thought themselves warranted to roar." Goldsmith reached the theatre only to hear a hiss (at the improbability of Mrs. Hardcastle, in her own garden, supposing herself at Crackskull Common). When he asked the reason, Colman replied, "Pshaw ! Doctor, don't be terrified at squibs when we have been sitting these two hours upon a barrel of gun powder."

However, the play was, contrary to Colman's apprehensions, a complete success. "Pit, boxes and galleries," says Macaulay, "were in a constant roar of laughter. If any bigoted admirer of Kelly and Cumberland ventured to hiss or groan, he was speedily silenced by a general cry of 'Turn him out', or 'throw him over.' Two generations have since confirmed the verdict which was pronounced on that night."[15]

Goldsmith's contemporaries such as Arthur Murphy, Charles Macklin, George Colman, David Garrick, Samuel Foote and R.B. Sheridan also worked in non-sentimental modes. The prologue for the tenth night of *The Rivals* (1775) clearly suggests Sheridan's opposition to the sentimental comedy. Pointing to the Figure of Comedy the speaker says:

Must we displace her ? And instead advance
The Goddess of the woeful countenance—
The Sentimental Muse !

These lines are remarkably similar to those in Garrick's brilliant prologue for *She Stoops to Conquer.* Moreover, Goldsmith does not seem to realise that sentimental comedy and laughing comedy may not be mutually exclusive. As Professor Friedman[16] observes, many of the plays which Goldsmith would apparently designate as "weeping sentimental comedies" were not intended to produce tears throughout and they do not contain too many sentimental scenes. The gloomy picture of the English comic drama drawn in Goldsmith's rhetorical "Essay" and in Garrick's prologue to *She Stoops to Conquer* is somewhat inaccurate.

Despite the vogue for sentimental comedy in Goldsmith's time, the laughing comedy was, as already pointed out, far from disappearing from the English stage. As Bevis[17] shows in his scholarly study of the afterpiece tradition, many of the eighteenth-century afterpieces are unsentimental and laughable. As regards the mainpieces, there are many satirical and laughing comedies of Goldsmith's contemporaries throughout the later 1750s and 1760s. These comedies often conform, if only in basic structure, to the comic pattern of Goldsmith's plays. Professor Quintana[18] rightly says that *She Stoops to Conquer* and *The Good-Natur'd Man* observe various conventions that governed the construction of many Georgian plays. Goldsmith's blend of satire, humours characters and geniality can also be found in the plays of Murphy, Colman and Garrick. Professor Hume[19] concurs with Quintana. Drawing upon the best of recent Goldsmith scholarship, he presents convincing evidence from the performance records in *The London Stage* to prove that in Goldsmith's time laughter and amusement were not being banished from the English stage.

Goldsmith was not, therefore, the only Georgian writer of laughing comedies. Nor did he really succeed in laying the ghost of sentimental comedy as it continued to be written and popular even after his death in 1774. But, as we have seen, Goldsmith was, as a dramatic critic, unusually conscientious, frank and consistent in his disapproval of sentimental comedy. His last strictures on sentimental comedy are contained in "Retaliation," the poem which he had written shortly before his death. Referring to the comic muse of the sentimental playwright, Cumberland, he writes: "Like a tragedy queen he has dizen'd her out,/Or rather like tragedy giving a rout." This parallels Goldsmith's criticism of sentimental comedy in his "Essay on the Theatre" where he affirmed that comedy lost its *raison d'etre* by substituting much of the pathetic for the truly comic.

Goldsmith seems to have been deeply disturbed by the popularity of the sentimental comedy in his time. He regretted that the contemporary critics, theatre-managers and audiences continued to admire this comedy despite its pathetic scenes, gushing sentiment and dull moralizing. His pronouncements against sentimental comedy and for genuine comedy help us to appreciate his own two comedies, written in accord with his theoretic ideals. As a dramatist Goldsmith countered this comedy with his truly laughing comedies. As this study shows, both *The Good-Natur'd Man* and *She Stoops to Conquer* are delightful because of their funny situations, witty dialogues, humorous characters and healthy spirit devoid of all sickly sensibility. The brilliance of *She Stoops to Conquer* suggests that Goldsmith's early death deprived us of a comic dramatist who might have risen to become the English Moliere. His main contribution to dramatic history lies in restoring to comedy much of its former élan.

NOTES

1. Goldsmith, as stated above, strongly disapproved of this particular form of disparagement on the part of the sentimentalists.
2. Mark Schorer, *MLN*, 48 (1933), pp. 91-94, suggests that Goldsmith was possibly influenced by a rather similar situation in Mrs. Centlivre's comedy, *The Man's Bewitch'd* (1709).
3. The previous act has prepared us for the joke.

4. These delightful asides, though designed for the intimate Covent Garden Stage of the time, are fully integrated with their situations.
5. This scene is obviously intended as a burlesque upon the insipid exchanges found in the plays of Hugh Kelly and Richard Cumberland.
6. Here Hastings is making use of Mrs. Hardcastle's ignorance of London because, as Professor Friedman points out, "St. James's clearly represents high life and Tower Wharf low life."
7. The elan of this scene alone is sufficient to keep the final happy union of Kate and Marlow free from any sentimentality.
8. Thorndike, p. 427.
9. Cited by G.S. Rousseau, ed., *Goldsmith: The Critical Heritage* (London, 1974), p. 331.
10. J. Forster, *The Life and Times of Oliver Goldsmith*, 2 vols. (London, 1877), II, 363 n., says that Lord Clare's daughter played this trick on Goldsmith.
11. Cited by Rousseau, *Goldsmith*, p. 118.
12. Thorndike, p. 429.
13. Cited by Rousseau, *Goldsmith*, p. 116.
14. Friedman, *Collected Works*, V, p. 89.
15. Cited by Rousseau, *Goldsmith*, p. 351.
16. A. Friedman, "Aspects of Sentimentalism in Eighteenth Century Literature," p. 252.
17. R.W. Bevis, "The Comic Tradition on the London Stage, 1737-77," unpub. diss. (Univ. of California, Berkeley, 1965).
18. Quintana, "Goldsmith's Achievement as Dramatist", p. 166.
19. R.D. Hume, "Goldsmith and Sheridan and the Supposed Revolution of 'Laughing' against 'sentimental' Comedy," *Studies in Change and Revolution*, ed. P. Korshin (London, 1972), p. 271.

List of Abbreviations

The following widely accepted abbreviations are used to indicate titles of learned journals:

CHEL	:	*The Cambridge History of English Literature*
EC	:	*Essays in Criticism*
ELH	:	*English Literary History*
E & S	:	*Essays and Studies by Members of the English Association*
JEGP	:	*Journal of English and Germanic Philology*
MLN	:	*Modern Language Notes*
MLQ	:	*Modern Language Quarterly*
MQ	:	*Modern Quarterly*
MP	:	*Modern Philology*
NQ	:	*Notes and Queries*
PMLA	:	*Publications of the Modern Language Association of America*
PQ	:	*Philological Quarterly*
RES	:	*Review of English Studies*
SAQ	:	*South Atlantic Quarterly*
SP	:	*Studies in Philology*
TLS	:	*The Times Literary Supplement*

Bibliography

The following list mentions, in alphabetical order, works consulted on particular points besides those cited in this study.

Texts

British Dramatists from Dryden to Sheridan. Ed. G.H. Nettleton and A.E. Case. London, 1939.

The Brothers by Richard Cumberland, in *The British Drama. London, 1871.*

The Collected Works of Oliver Goldsmith. Ed. A. Friedman. 5 vols. Oxford, 1966.

Comedies by William Congreve. Ed. B. Dobree. World's Classics, 1925; rpt. London, 1969.

The Complete Works and Poems of Sir George Etherege. Ed. A.W. Verity. London, 1888.

The Complete Works of George Farquhar. Ed. C. Stonehill. 2 vols. Bloomsbury, 1930.

The Dramatic Works of Colley Cibber. 5 vols. London, 1777.

The Dramatic Works of Sir George Etherege. Ed. H.F.B. Brett-Smith. 2 vols. Oxford, 1927.

Eighteenth Century Comedy. Ed. W.D. Taylor. World's Classics, 1929.

Eighteenth Century Plays. Ed. J. Hampden. Everyman's Library, 1928.

James Boswell, The Life of Samuel Johnson. Ed. George Birkbeck Hill and L.F. Powell. 6 vols. Oxford, 1934-50.

The Miscellaneous Works of Oliver Goldsmith. Ed. D. Masson. Globe Edition. London, 1918.

Oliver Goldsmith: Poems and Plays. Everyman's Edition, 1910; rpt. London, 1974.

Plays of the Restoration and Eighteenth Century. Ed. D. MacMillan and H.M. Jones. New York, 1931.

The Plays of Richard Steele. Ed. S.S. Kenny. Oxford, 1971.

Richard Steele. Ed. G.A. Aitken. Mermaid Series. London, 1894.

The Runaway, A Comedy by Mrs. Cowley: As it is Acted at the Theatre-Royal in Drury-Lane. London, 1776.

The School for Rakes, A Comedy by Mrs. Elizabeth Griffiths. London, 1795.

The School for Wives, in *The Modern Theatre: A Collection of Successful Modern Plays...Selected by Mrs. Inchbald*. 10 vols. London, 1811.

Selections from The Tatler and The Spectator of Steele and Addison. Ed. Angus Ross. London and New York, 1982.

Shaftesbury, A.A. Cooper, Third Earl of. *Characteristics of Men, Manners, Opinions, Times*. 3 vols. London, 1727.

Sir John Vanbrugh. Ed. W.C. Ward. 2 vols. London, 1893.

Twelve Famous Plays of the Restoration and Eighteenth Century. Ed. C.A. Moore. New York, 1933.

Whitehead, William. *The School for Lovers: A Comedy, As it is Acted at the Theatre-Royal in Drury-Lane By His Majesty's Servants*. London, 1762.

The Works of Joseph Addison. Ed. R. Hurd. London, 1873.

Critical and Biographical Studies

Alderman, W.E. "Shaftesbury and the Doctrine of Moral Sense in the Eighteenth Century." *PMLA*, 46 (1931).

———. "Shaftesbury and the Doctrine of Benevolence in the Eighteenth Century." *Transactions of the Wisconsin Academy of Sciences, Arts and Letters*, 26 (1931).

Aldridge, A.O. "The Pleasures of Pity." *ELH*, 16 (1949).

Allen, B. Sprague. "The Dates of *Sentimental* and Its Derivatives." *PMLA*, 48 (1933).

Allen, R.J. *Life in Eighteenth-Century England.* Boston, 1941.

Anthony, R. *The Jeremy Collier Stage Controversy*. Milwaukee, 1937.

Avery, E.L. et. al. Eds. *The London Stage, 1660-1800*. 11 vols. Carbondale, I ll, 1960-68.

Babcock, R.W. "Benevolence, Sensibility and Sentiment in Eighteenth Century Periodicals." *MLN*, 42 (1947).

Bahlman, Dudley W.R. *The Moral Revolution of 1688*. London, 1957.

Baker, E.A. *The History of the English Novel.* Vols. IV-V. London, 1927-30.

Barbauld, A.L. Ed. *The Correspondence of Samuel Richardson.* London, 1959.

Bateson, F.W. *English Comic Drama, 1700-1750*. New York, 1963.

———. "L.C. Knights and Restoration Comedy." *EC*, 7 (1957).

Battestin, M.C. "Fielding and Ralph Allen: Benevolism and Its Limits as an Eighteenth Century Ideal." *MLQ*, 28 (September 1967).

Bear, A. "Restoration Comedy and the Provok'd Critic," *Restoration Literature: Critical Approaches*, ed. H. Love, London, 1972.

Bergson, H. *Laughter.* Tr. C. Brereton and F. Rothwell. London, 1935.

Berkeley, D.S. "The Penitent Rake in Restoration Comedy." *MP*, 49 (1952).

Bernbaum, E. *The Drama of Sensibility*. Boston, 1915.

Bevis, R.W. "The Comic Tradition on the London Stage, 1737-77." unpub. diss. Univ. of California, Berkeley, 1965.

———. Ed. *Eighteenth Century Drama: Afterpieces*. London, 1970.

———. *The Laughing Tradition: Stage Comedy in Garrick's Day*. University of Georgia Press, 1980.

Birkhead, E. "Sentiment and Sensibility in the Eighteenth Century Novel." *E & S*, 11 (1925).

Boas, F.S. *An Introduction to Eighteenth Century Drama.* Oxford, 1953.

Brauer, G.C. "Good Breeding in the Eighteenth Century." *University of Texas Studies in English*, 32 (1953).

Bredvold, L.I. "The Literature of the Restoration and the Eighteenth Century," *A History of English Literature*, ed. H. Craig. New York, 1950.

Bredvold, L.J. *The Natural History of Sensibility.* Detroit, 1962.

Brett, R.L. *The Third Earl of Shaftesbury: A Study in Eighteenth Century Literary Theory.* London, 1951.

Butcher, S.H. *Aristotle's Theory of Poetry and Fine Art.* Dover Publications, 1951.

Butt, J. *The Augustan Age.* London, 1950.

Calverton, V.F. "Social Change and the Sentimental Comedy." *MQ* (1925).

Caskey, J.H. "Arthur Murphy and the War on Sentimental Comedy." *JEGP*, 30 (1931).

———. *The Life and Works of Edward Moore.* New Haven, 1927.

Cecil, C.D. "Libertine and Precieux Elements in Restoration Comedy." *EC*, 9 (1959).

Chapin, C. "Shaftesbury and the Man of Feeling." *MP*, 81 (August 1983).

Cibber, C. *An Apology for His Life.* London, 1914.

Clark, W.K.L. *Eighteenth-Century Piety.* London, 1944.

Clifford, J.L. Ed. *Eighteenth Century English Literature: Modern Essays in Criticism.* New York, 1959.

Collins, P.A.W. "Restoration Comedy," *From Dryden to Johnson*, ed. Boris Ford, Penguin Books, 1957.

Connoly, L.W. *Brawny Wycherley.* New York, 1930.

———. *The Censorship of English Drama, 1737-1824.* London, 1976.

Cooper, L. *Aristotle on the Art of Poetry.* New York, 1947.

———, *An Aristotelian Theory of Comedy.* New York, 1922.

Corman, B. "What is Restoration Drama ?" *University of Toronto Quarterly*, 48 (1978).

Crane, R.S. "Suggestions toward a Genealogy of the 'Man of Feeling'. " *ELH*, 1 (1934).

Crawford, B.V. "High Comedy in Terms of Restoration Practice." *PQ*, 8 (1929).

Croissant, De Witt C. "Early Sentimental Comedy." *Essays on Dramatic Literature: The Parrott Presentation Volume*, ed. H. Craig. Princeton, 1935.

———. *Studies in the Work of Colley Cibber.* Lawrence, Kan., 1912.

Daiches, D. *A Critical History of English Literature.* 2 vols. London, 1961.

———. *Critical Approaches to Literature.* New Delhi, 1967.

Danziger, M.K. *Oliver Goldsmith and Richard Brinsley Sheridan.* New York, 1978.

Detisch, R.J. "The Synthesis of Laughing and Sentimental Comedy in *The West Indian*." *Educational Theatre Journal*, 22 (October 1970).

Dibdin, C. *A Complete History of the Stage.* London, 1795.

Dobree, B. *English Literature in the Early Eighteenth Century, 1700-1740.* Oxford, 1959.

———. *Restoration Comedy, 1660-1720.* Oxford, 1958.

Dodds, J.W. *Thomas Southerne, Dramatist.* New Haven, Conn., 1933.

Donohue, Jr. *Dramatic Character in the English Romantic Age.* Princeton, 1970.

Draper, J.W. "Theory of Comic in Eighteenth Century England." *JEGP*, 37 (1938).

Drew, Elizabeth. *Discovering Drama.* New York, 1937.

Durham, W.H. Ed. *Critical Essays of the Eighteenth Century, 1700-1725.* New York, 1961.

Edmunds, J.M. "An example of Early Sentimentalism." *MLN*, 48 (1933).

Elton, O. *A Survey of English Literature, 1730-1780.* 2 vols. London, 1959.

Enright, D.J. and Chickera, E. De. Eds. *English Critical Texts.* London, 1970.

Essays on the Eighteenth Century Presented to D.N. Smith. Oxford, 1945.

Evans, A.A. "The Impact of Rousseau on English Education." *Researches and Studies,* 11 (1955).

Ferguson, O.W. "Goldsmith." *SAQ,* 66 (1967).

———. "Kelly vs. Goldsmith: The Bailiffs in *The School for Wives.*" *Theatre Survey,* 19 (1978).

———. "Antisentimentalism in Goldsmith's *The Good Natur'd Man*: The Limits of Parody," *The Dress of Words,* ed. Robert B. White, Jr. University of Kansas Libraries, 1978.

———. "Oliver Goldsmith: The Personality of the Essayist." *PQ,* 61 (Spring 1982).

———. "Goldsmith's 'Retaliation'." *SAQ,* 70 (Spring 1971).

Ford, B. Ed. *From Dryden to Johnson.* Penguin Books, 1957.

Forster, J. *The Life and Times of Oliver Goldsmith.* London, 1877.

Friedman, A. "Aspects of Sentimentalism in Eighteenth Century Literature." *The Augustan Milieu. . .* ed. H.K. Miller, E. Rothstein and G.S. Rousseau. Oxford, 1970.

Frye, N. "Towards Defining an Age of Sensibility." *ELH,* 23 (June 1956).

Fujimura, T.H. *The Restoration Comedy of Wit.* Princeton, 1952.

Gagan, J. "Congreve's Mirabell and the Ideal of the Gentleman." *PMLA,* 79 (1964).

Gallaway Jr., W.F. "The Sentimentalism of Goldsmith." *PMLA,* 48 (1933).

Garnett, R. *The Age of Dryden.* London, 1932.

Gassner, J. *Masters of the Drama.* Dover Publications, 1954.

Genest, J. *Some Account of the English Stage from 1660.* 10 vols. Bath, 1832.

Ginger, J. *The Notable Man: The Life and Times of Oliver Goldsmith* London, 1977.

George, M.D. *English Social Life in the Eighteenth Century.* London, 1923.

Gosse, E. *A History of Eighteenth Century English Literature.* New York, 1927.

Green, J.R. *A Short History of the English People.* 2 vols. London, 1926.

Greig, J.Y.T. *The Psychology of Laughter and Comedy.* London, 1923.

Griffin, R.J. "Goldsmith's Augustanism: A Study of His Literary Works." unpub. diss., Univ. of California, Berkeley, 1965.

Hagstrum, J.H. *Samuel Johnson's Literary Criticism.* Minneapolis, Minn., 1952.

Hare, M.E. "Steele and Sentimental Comedy," *Eighteenth Century Literature: An Oxford Miscellany.* London, 1909.

Hartnoll, P. Ed. *The Oxford Companion to the Theatre.* London, 1951.

Hazard, P. *European Thought in the Eighteenth Century.* London, 1954.

Hazlitt, W. *Lectures on the English Comic Writers,* London, 1819.

Heilman, R.B. "The Sentimentalism of Goldsmith's *Good-Natur'd Man,*" *Studies for William A. Read* Baton Rouge, 1940.

Helgerson, R. "The Two Worlds of Oliver Goldsmith." *Studies in English Literature,* 13 (1973).

Holland, N.N. *The First Modern Comedies.* Bloomington and London, 1967.

Hooker, E.N. Ed. *The Critical Works of John Dennis.* 2 vols. Baltimore, 1939-43.

Hopes, J. "Politics and Morality in the Writings of Jeremy Collier." *Literature and History,* 8 (1978).

Hopkins, R.H. *The True Genius of Oliver Goldsmith.* Baltimore, 1969.

Houghton, W.E. "Lamb's Criticism of Restoration Comedy." *ELH,* 10 (1943).

Hume, R.D. "Goldsmith and Sheridan and the Supposed Revolution of 'Laughing' against 'Sentimental' Comedy," *Studies in Change and Revolution*, ed. P.J. Korshin. Menston, 1972.

———. "Theory of Comedy in the Restoration." *MP*, 70 (1972-73).

———. *The Development of English Drama in the Late Seventeenth Century*. Oxford, 1976.

———. "The Myth of the Rake in 'Restoration' Comedy." *Studies in the Literary Imagination*, 10 (1977).

———. "*English Drama and Theatre 1660-1800*: New Directions in Research." *Theatre Survey*, 23 (May 1982).

———. *The Rakish Stage: Studies in English Drama, 1660-1800*. Carbondale and Edwardsville, 1983.

Humphreys, A.R. *The Augustan World*. London, 1954.

———. " 'The Friend of Mankind' (177-1760) an aspect of Eighteenth Century Sensibility." *RES*, 24 (1948).

Jeffares, A.N. *Oliver Goldsmith*, London, 1965.

Jordan, R. "The Extravagant Rake in Restoration Comedy," *Restoration Literature: Critical Approaches*, ed. H. Love. London, 1972.

Kaul, A.N. *The Action of English Comedy: Studies in the Encounter of Abstraction and Experience from Shakespeare to Shaw*. Delhi, 1970.

Kenny, S.S. "Richard Steele and the 'Pattern of Genteel Comedy'." *MP*, 70 (1972).

———. "Humane Comedy." *MP*, 75 (1977).

Ker, W.P. "On Comedy," *On Modern Literature*. . . ed. T. Spencer and J. Sutherland. Oxford, 1955.

Kies, P.P. "Lessing's Relation to Early English Sentimental Comedy." *PMLA*, 47 (1932).

Knights, L.C. "Restoration Comedy: The Reality and the Myth," *Explorations*. London. 1946.

Krutch, J.W. *Comedy and Conscience After the Restoration*. New York, 1924.

Lamb, C. "On the Artificial Comedy of the Last Century," *Complete Works and Letters of Charles Lamb.* The Modern Library, 1935.

Leech, C. "Restoration Comedy: The Earlier Phase." *EC,* 1 (1951).

———. "Congreve and the Century's End." *PQ,* 41 (1962).

Loftis, J. *Comedy and Society from Congreve to Fielding.* Stanford, 1959.

———. Ed. *Restoration Drama: Modern Essays in Criticism.* New York, 1966.

Love, H. "The Myth of the Restoration Audience," *Komos,* 2 (1967).

Lucas, F.L. *The Search for Good Sense: Four Eighteenth Century Characters, Johnson, Chesterfield, Boswell, Goldsmith.* London, 1958.

Lynch, K.M. *The Social Mode of Restoration Comedy.* New York, 1975.

———. "Thomas D'Urfey's Contribution to Sentimental Comedy." *PQ,* 9 (1930).

Macaulay, Lord T.B. "The Comic Dramatists of the Restoration," *Critical and Historical Essays.* Everyman's Library, 1843.

Marwin, M. "Restoration Comedy and Later," *English Stage Comedy,* ed. W.K. Wimsatt, Jr. London, 1955.

Mayo, R.D. *The English Novel in the Magazines, 1740-1815.* London, 1962.

McCarthy, B.E. "The Theme of Liberty in *She Stoops to Conquer.*" *Univ. of Windsor Review,* 7 (1971).

McDonald, Charles O. "Restoration Comedy as Drama of Satire: An Investigation into Seventeenth Century Aesthetics." *SP,* 61 (1964).

Meredith, G. *An Essay on Comedy and the Uses of the Comic Spirit.* London, 1910.

Moore, C.A. "Shaftesbury and the Ethical Poets in England, 1700-1760." *PMLA,* 31 (1916).

Mueschke, P. and Jeannette, F. "A Re-evaluation of Vanbrugh." *PMLA*, 49 (1934).

Muir, K. *The Comedy of Manners*. London, 1970.

Mumford, W. *The Life of Richard Cumberland*. 2 vols. London, 1812.

Needham, H.A. Ed. *Taste and Criticism in the Eighteenth Century*. London, 1952.

Nettleton, G.H. "The Drama and the Stage." *CHEL*, 10 (1912).

———. *English Drama of the Restoration and Eighteenth Century*. New York, 1914.

Nicoll, A. *A History of Restoration Drama, 1660-1700*. Cambridge, 1923.

———. *A History of Early Eighteenth Century Drama, 1700-1750*. Cambridge, 1925.

———. *A History of Late Eighteenth Century Drama, 1750-1800*. Cambridge, 1927.

———. *The Theory of Drama*. London, 1931.

———. *British Drama*. London, 1951.

———. *The Theatre and Dramatic Theory*. London, 1962.

Palmer, J. *The Comedy of Manners*. London, 1913.

Parnell, Paul E. "The Sentimental Mask." *PMLA*, 78 (1963).

Perry, H.T.E. *The Comic Spirit in Restoration Drama*. New Haven, 1925.

Pinto, V. de S. *Restoration Carnival*. London, 1954.

Porter, R. *English Society in the Eighteenth Century*. London and New York, 1982.

Potts, L.J. *Comedy*. London. 1948.

Preston, T.R. "Smollett and the Benevolent Misanthrope Type." *PMLA*, 79 (March 1964).

Quintana, R. "Goldsmith's Achievement as Dramatist." *Univ. of Toronto Quarterly*, 34 (1965).

———. *Oliver Goldsmith: A Georgian Study*. London, 1967.

Rawson, C.J. "Some Remarks on Eighteenth Century 'Delicacy' with a Note on Hugh Kelly's *False Delicacy* (1768)." *JEGP*, 61 (1962).

Reed, R.R. "James Shirley and the Sentimental Comedy." *Anglia*, 73 (1955).

———. "Ben Jonson's Pioneering in Sentimental Comedy." *NQ*, 195 (1950).

Ristine, F.H. *English Tragicomedy*. New York, 1910.

Rodway, A. "Goldsmith and Sheridan: Satirists of Sentiment," "*Renaissance and Modern Essays Presented to Vivian de Sola Pinto*, ed. G.R. Hibbard. London, 1966.

Rousseau, G.S. Ed. *Goldsmith: The Critical Heritage*. London, 1974.

Saintsbury, G. *The Peace of the Augustans*. World's Classics, 1946.

Schelling, F.E. "The Restoration Drama." *CHEL*, Vol. VIII, 1932.

Scheurer, C.M. "An Early Sentimental Comedy." *Anglia*, 37 (1913).

Schorer, M. "Hugh Kelly: His Place in the Sentimental School." *PQ*, 12 (October 1933).

Shepherd, T.B. *Methodism and the Literature of the Eighteenth Century*. London, 1940.

Sherbo, A. *English Sentimental Drama*. East Lansing, Mich., 1957.

Sherburn, G. "The Restoration and Eighteenth Century, 1660-1789," *A Literary History of England*, ed. A.C. Baugh. London, 1950.

Smith, J.H. *The Gay Couple in Restoration Comedy*. Cambridge. Mass., 1948.

———. "Shadwell, The Ladies, and the Change in Comedy." *MP*, 46 (1948).

Smith, W. *The Nature of Comedy*. Boston, 1930.

Spingarn, J.E. Ed. *Critical Essays of the Seventeenth Century*. 3 vols, Oxford, 1908-9.

Stein, Elizabeth P. *David Garrick, Dramatist*. New York. 1938.

Stephen, Sir Leslie. *English Literature and Society in the Eighteenth Century*. London, 1904.

NOTES

ज्ञान गरिमा के
72 वर्ष

भारतीय
ज्ञानपीठ